THE TEARS OF THE BLACK MAN

GLOBAL AFRICAN VOICES

Dominic Thomas, *Editor*

I Was an Elephant Salesman:
Adventures between Dakar,
Paris, and Milan
Pap Khouma, Edited by Oreste
Pivetta
Translated by Rebecca Hopkins
Introduction by Graziella Parati

Little Mother: A Novel
Cristina Ali Farah
Translated by Giovanna
Bellesia-Contuzzi and Victoria
Offredi Poletto
Introduction by Alessandra
Di Maio

Life and a Half: A Novel
Sony Labou Tansi
Translated by Alison Dundy
Introduction by Dominic Thomas

Transit: A Novel
Abdourahman A. Waberi
Translated by David Ball and
Nicole Ball

Cruel City: A Novel
Mongo Beti
Translated by Pim Higginson

Blue White Red: A Novel
Alain Mabanckou
Translated by Alison Dundy

The Past Ahead: A Novel
Gilbert Gatore
Translated by Marjolijn de Jager

Queen of Flowers and Pearls:
A Novel
Gabriella Ghermandi
Translated by Giovanna
Bellesia-Contuzzi and Victoria
Offredi Poletto

The Shameful State: A Novel
Sony Labou Tansi
Translated by Dominic Thomas
Foreword by Alain Mabanckou

Kaveena
Boubacar Boris Diop
Translated by Bhakti
Shringarpure and
Sara C. Hanaburgh

Murambi, The Book of Bones
Boubacar Boris Diop
Translated by Fiona Mc Laughlin

The Heart of the Leopard
Children
Wilfried N'Sondé
Translated by Karen Lindo

Harvest of Skulls
Abdourahman A. Waberi
Translated by Dominic Thomas

Jazz and Palm Wine
Emmanuel Dongala
Translated by Dominic Thomas

The Silence of the Spirits
Wilfried N'Sondé
Translated by Karen Lindo

Congo Inc.: Bismarck's Testament
In Koli Jean Bofane
Translated by Marjolijn de Jager

Concrete Flowers
Wilfried N'Sondé
Translated by Karen Lindo

THE TEARS
OF THE BLACK MAN

Alain Mabanckou

Translated by Dominic Thomas

Indiana University Press

This book is a publication of

Indiana University Press
Office of Scholarly Publishing
Herman B Wells Library 350
1320 East 10th Street
Bloomington, Indiana 47405 USA

iupress.indiana.edu

First published as *Le Sanglot de l'Homme Noir* by Éditions Fayard © 2012
English translation © 2018 by Indiana University Press
All rights reserved

The paper used in this publication meets the minimum requirements
of the American National Standard for Information Sciences—
Permanence of Paper for Printed Library Materials, ANSI Z39.48-1992.

Manufactured in the United States of America

Cataloging information is available from the Library of Congress.

ISBN 978-0-253-03583-7 (pbk.)
ISBN 978-0-253-03585-1 (MOBI)
ISBN 978-0-253-03584-4 (web PDF)
ISBN 978-0-253-03586-8 (ePub)

1 2 3 4 5   23 22 21 20 19 18

What's all this about black people and a black nationality? ... I take a personal interest in the destiny of France, the French nation, and its values. What am I supposed to do with a black empire?

—Frantz Fanon, *Black Skin, White Masks*[1]

---

1 Frantz Fanon, *Black Skin, White Masks*, translated by Richard Philcox (New York: Grove Press, 2008 [1952]), 179.

Contents*

1. The Black Man's Tears (Pascal Bruckner)   *1*

2. A Negro in Paris (Bernard Dadié)   *6*

3. The Spirit of the Laws (Montesquieu)   *14*

4. Murderous Identities (Amin Maalouf)   *18*

5. Road to Europe (Ferdinand Oyono)   *27*

6. How Can One Be Persian? (Montesquieu)   *32*

7. The Foreign Student (Philippe Labro)   *36*

8. Bound to Violence (Yambo Ouologuem)   *44*

9. The Identity Card (Jean-Marc Adiaffi)   *51*

10. Literature of the Stomach (Julien Gracq)   *53*

11. Phantom Africa (Michel Leiris)   *58*

12. The Suns of Independence (Ahmadou Kourouma)   *63*

    Appendix   *69*
    Notes   *71*

---

*Individual chapter headings in the original French version of this book were borrowed from existing works by authors whose names are included in parentheses. In this version, the titles of published translations were used when available, or adapted for the purposes of clarity in individual chapters.

THE TEARS OF THE BLACK MAN

1 The Black Man's Tears

Dear Boris,

Relations between France and Africa are difficult to explain. Your school textbooks will no doubt have taught you more on this subject than I will ever be able to, but it is safe to say that this long history has been marked by dramatic ups and downs. There are those who will try and convince you to bear a grudge against France, to blame her for all the suffering. As for me, I'm with those who believe that Africa's history has yet to be written. This will require patience and serenity, and one should avoid tipping the scales in favor of a particular version of history. Others call for a more vigorous response from Africa itself, and since the dark continent is still considered the cradle of humanity, these same people will try and convince you in their zeal that Europe should just give in and agree to reparations as a remedy for all the damage they inflicted on us during the centuries of slavery, the decades of colonization, and God knows what else.

In *The Tears of the White Man*, French philosopher Pascal Bruckner talked about the "self-loathing" felt by Europeans, the feeling of culpability that comes from the self-hatred and contempt they experience when they look back on their history, especially colonialism and capitalism.[1] Their bad conscience distorts their perception of the Third World, redirecting them toward leftist, naive, Manichean views. This is their way of *repenting* and seeking salvation. Rather than being continually filled with a futile sense of *repentance*, Bruckner urges Europeans to be proud of their accomplishments.

Slightly altering the philosopher's title, I believe there is ample evidence today of what I would describe as "the tears of the black man." Tears that are becoming increasingly noisy and driving some Africans to attribute all the continent's sufferings and misfortunes to the encounter with Europe. These tearful Africans relentlessly fuel hatred toward Whites, as if vengeance could somehow erase the history of ignominy and give us back the alleged pride Europe violated. But those who blindly hate Europe are just as sick as those who cling to a blind love for a bygone, imaginary Africa, one that somehow survived the centuries peacefully, seamlessly, until that fateful day when the Whites came along and turned their perfect world upside down.

These tearful Blacks claim to be followers of Marcus Garvey, who initiated the Back to Africa movement for the descendants of slaves, or of the great Senegalese historian Cheikh Anta Diop, who argued relentlessly that ancient Egypt had been populated by Black people and that Western philosophers had plundered African thought shamelessly since Antiquity. In their state of trance, they tirelessly dwell on the key ideas of "black consciousness" and of the "African renaissance." To this end, they summon Elijah Muhammad (the former leader of the Nation of Islam), or, for that matter, Malcolm X, who was his spiritual son for a while. Similarly, they never fail to mention the main Pan-Africanists of the Black continent—Kwame Nkrumah and Amílcar Cabral—or the warrior Shaka Zulu, who conquered a huge empire in southern Africa that was larger than France. But they will neglect to mention that the legendary warrior later became a despot responsible for the deaths of several million Africans during his tyrannical rule.

Most likely you'll be surprised to hear Martin Luther King Jr.'s name mentioned, a relentless advocate of nonviolence, because these tearful Blacks don't think twice when it comes to distorting and amalgamating ideas and concepts that are in reality far more subtle and different than they are willing to admit.

"Black consciousness" is, when it comes down to it, a *demonstration* rather than a *construction*, so that one doesn't have to expend too much energy in "making an assessment of black values," as Frantz Fanon once wrote.[2] In some respects, this is tantamount to a pure and simple demolition of the man of color who, rather than focusing on the present, ends up being sidetracked in the meanders of a past encompassed by legends, myth, and above all else, "nostalgia."

These same tearful Blacks are convinced that our very survival is premised on the annihilation of the White race or, at the very least, by reversing our historical roles. In their opinion, Whites should be made to feel, even for a few hours, what it means to be Black in this world. Yet, in their unconscious, as Fanon claimed, they have always harbored dreams of actually being White: "The black man wants to be like the white man? For the black man, there is but one destiny. And it is white. A long time ago the black man acknowledged the undeniable superiority of the white man, and all his endeavors aim at achieving a white existence."[3] In fact, the Martinican psychiatrist went on to ask: "Haven't I got better things to do on this earth than avenge the Blacks of the seventeenth century?"[4] And for those who continue to lament the Black continent's bygone glory days, Fanon's conclusion in *Black Skin, White Masks* remains more valid today than ever: "Above all, let there be no misunderstanding. We are convinced that it would be of enormous interest to discover a black literature or architecture from the third century before Christ. We would be overjoyed to learn of the existence of a correspondence between some black philosopher and Plato. But we can absolutely not see how this fact would change the life of eight-year-old kids working in the cane fields of Martinique."[5]

My dear boy, the worst forms of intolerance always come from your own people, from those whose skin color is closest to your own. Fanaticism first rears its ugly head among those of the same origin, only later extending toward those of the other "races," and with a virulence nourished by a spirit of vengeance.

I used to spend hours listening to the Black activists preaching on the Esplanade outside the Centre Pompidou when I was studying law in Paris during the nineties. Cheikh Anta Diop was regularly summoned in their speeches, although few among them had actually ever read his work. Convinced as they were of being disciples of the Senegalese historian—even though his thinking was based on science and the desire to better understand the Black continent—they were hell-bent on igniting a race war. Demagogic propagandists who had come too late now pressed White people to kneel and recognize Black civilization's precedence. The more I thought about these arguments, the more I found their way of clinging to the primacy of origins annoying.

The challenge for you, my son, is to figure out what this "primacy" has to offer but also how it may be potentially limiting, since you must act in the present and think about your future as well as that of your own descendants. Tearful Africans claim they were here first. My response to them is: Good for you! And then I follow up with a question that usually derails them: Now what?

In France, where you were born and live, I can't think of any "black consciousness" movement that has grabbed hold of the present, because our "activists" are still looking in the rear-view mirror. And in so doing, they have forged a union based on a mythical past rather than establishing something new based on everyday preoccupations. Hidden behind these factionalist ideologies lies an indirect appeal for pity for Black people. But the salvation of Black people is not to be found in commiseration or humanitarian aid. If that was all that was needed, well then, all the wretched of the earth would already have altered the course of history. It is no longer enough to claim to be Black or to shout it from the rooftops in order for four centuries of humiliation to flash through the other's mind. It is no longer enough to hail from the Global South and demand assistance from the prosperous North. Because that assistance is nothing less than the surreptitious continuation of subjugation.

Furthermore, to say that one is Black doesn't really mean much these days. As long as Blacks sit back waiting for salvation to come from commiseration, their only interlocutors with be their own brothers—more often than not overlooking the fact that their nations have been independent since the sixties, preferring instead to spew forth in the way of false prophets anointed to speak in the name of a Black community that doesn't exist in France. And, when it comes down to it, on what grounds?

In my book *Letter to Jimmy*, I pointed out how Africans basically don't know each other.[6] Africa is so diverse and fragmented, and cultures are not automatically the same from one country to the next. Advocates of colonialism could very well argue that Europe made it possible for different populations on the African continent to communicate, since in order to understand one another, most Africans today use the languages they inherited from their former masters. Blacks living in France, in Europe even, are strangers to one other; they don't have a shared consciousness founded on any kind of *logic* other than skin color, or a sense of belonging to the same continent or Black diaspora. Black Americans were at least able to develop such a consciousness over a long and tumultuous history. They became aware of the fact that the land on which they had ended up stranded and in chains would ultimately be the space in which they would have to fight for acceptance in order to finally become Americans. This is why the very idea of a Black community built on a past rather than on the lived *experience* on French soil, with the French people, is nothing else but a pipe dream welded together by regression and withdrawal. Some have advocated for establishing a community in France that would follow the example of Black Americans, but those folks are misguided, preferring to take a shortcut rather than consider how France is not the same. Their anemia, which has been simmering for a long time and become muddled with the hardships of daily life, has been handed down from one generation to the next. I wrote you this missive as a wake-up call, because I wouldn't want you to fall into that trap. You were born here, your destiny is here, and you should not lose sight of that fact. Ask yourself what you bring to this country without expecting to receive any rewards in return. That is the nature of the world. Real courage is doing the right thing when nobody is looking.

Your Father.

2 A Negro in Paris

DURING THE SUMMER months, I like to work out in a gym over in the twelfth arrondissement, up toward the Place de la Nation. Admittedly, it's a fairly unassuming place, but all the available equipment makes up for this. Unlike most of the facilities scattered all over the capital where folks often have to wait in line to use the machines, often going home frustrated, this place is much less crowded. The staff in the reception area are very lively and eager to sign you up with a personal trainer. At first, I found it hard to turn them down, and only a bit later when I let them know that someone was "taking care of me in the United States" did the manager give up, but not without adding:

"Ah! Those Americans! They're always one step ahead! Everyone has a *body trainer* over there! If we mention their services here, people just think we're trying to pull a fast one! Look at Jennifer Lopez's or Beyoncé's butts! Don't come and tell me they don't have specialists taking care of them! And take a look at some of our performers!"

The street level is reserved for cardio workouts and the first floor for *body-building*, and that's where the fitness instructors do the rounds trying to sign up new customers. That's also where some members, proud of the results they have achieved, now spend more time admiring themselves in the mirrors than actually working out. They wander around, shirtless, convinced they're the bee's knees. As soon as a woman comes into their vicinity, the competition intensifies. It's down to who can do the most challenging exercise. And let's not forget those who suddenly transform into altruists eager to help young women optimize their workout under the envious looks of their more timid rivals.

I get it: after having suffered so much, what greater reward than to show off the results? And as far as the owners are concerned, it's free advertising ...

One day, while I was busy trying to figure out how to use a new leg machine, a dark-skinned man came up to me. My first thought was that he was an employee coming to assist me. I was mistaken, since without so much as an opening greeting, he launched right in:

"Are you that Congolese guy I've seen a few times on TV talking about your novel? Aren't you the one who wrote a story about a porcupine?"

"That's me."

"And what's your name again?"

I introduced myself, but he didn't seem convinced.

"No, the guy I'm talking about always wears a cap! If that's you, then where's your cap?"

"I don't wear it when I'm working out, and ..."

Now come on brother, don't try and fool me! Where's your cap?"

"It's in my locker upstairs."

He pondered the situation, clearly trying to find a way to catch me out.

"Okay then, so your cap is in your locker! But the real problem is that the Congolese writer lives in America! What on earth would he be doing in this place?"

Somewhat annoyed, I said:

"I can't help it if you don't believe me."

"Come on now, cool it ... Do you have your membership card on you?"

I got my card out of my pocket and the man almost snatched it out of my hand. Then, exulting:

"It's really you!"

From that moment on he was unstoppable:

"It's a real pleasure to meet you. You know, I'm not boasting, but I really do enjoy reading. I've been reading since I was a child, but I'm so busy these days I barely have a minute to myself. France can do that to you at times, the country of Proust and Zola. I can still recite Vigny's *The Death of the Wolf* from memory, and I learned it back in high school! In any case, all that's a long time ago, and I don't really want to read what people are writing these days. In my opinion, writers do all they can today to make sure no one wants to read them! Am I wrong about that? All they're interested in are their lives instead of writing about ours!"

"Let's not get carried away, my brother, there are lots of good writers today, and ..."

"Who? Which writers? Those that go on TV to tell you how much they hate their parents? Do you think I'm going to sit down and read those kinds of books to my kids? Is that what being a writer is? I'm telling you, French literature is dead!"

I really didn't want to continue with this conversation. I withdrew and concentrated on the exercise I was doing. But my Black brother didn't budge, and just stood there watching me exert myself.

"I haven't introduced myself . . . I'm from the Central African region and have been living in France for several years. Let's say twenty-nine and a half years. All my children were born here, my brother. They are, how should I say, little French people, with nothing to do with Africa, a place they have never set foot. They are from here, period. But is that what the French think when they see them in school and in the streets? To them, they're just little Negroes."

I was sweating more and more profusely and had finally figured out how to use the machine.

"You're one of the lucky ones, my brother, hidden away in the United States where Blacks are at least respected, whereas over here the Blacks of France are still at the back of the line in Europe. I read somewhere on the internet that you were a university professor! Do you think you'd have found a position like that if you'd stayed here? Answer me, my brother! Am I wrong?"

"Well, let's just say that . . ."

"No, my brother, how many Blacks are professors in French universities?"

"Well, I have a couple of colleagues here and there who . . ."

"And where do they come from? And even if that were the case, are two or three enough when compared to the number of Blacks who graduate from French universities? Those two or three Blacks of France you know in universities, that's merely smoke, and they're probably part-time lecturers or something along those lines! They're there for the time being because there are no Whites available. But as soon as they show up, they won't think twice about firing them!"

"That's a bit of a generalization!"

"I'm only saying what's true, my brother! A Black person can NEVER be a real prof in a big university in this country! Those two or three colleagues you mentioned, let me tell you what they're there for: they're good for appearances, and that's about it! It's what I call the tree that hides the big forest! I for one studied literature for years in Paris, I wanted to be a teacher, but I waited in vain. Because the real

French, I mean the Whites, they all got to go in front of me, even the spotty-faced dropouts! And so I gave up, and today I do the dirty work France reserves for its Negroes!"

This time, I stopped pedaling.

"France has jobs it reserves for the Blacks?"

"Yes, my brother, you're cut off from the realities in this country, but what I'm telling you, all the Negroes in this country know it and will say the same thing! If you don't believe me, let's go outside and find a Black guy, and you'll see what he has to say ..."

"And just what is this job reserved for the Blacks of France?"

"Security!"

Trying my best not to laugh, I told him:

"Hold on now, lots of Black people in the US say the same thing about their country and ..."

"No, it's not the same thing over there! I know what I'm talking about!"

"So you've lived in America then?"

"No, but one of my cousins lives in Chicago and he told me that over there, Blacks can be bank managers even if they have dreadlocks like Yannick Noah or wear earrings like Bernard Lavilliers! You're not about to see that in France any time soon! I'd rather be Black over there than here! No comparison! Our American brothers have taken gigantic steps! Do you know what area I work in?"

He was quiet for a moment and then, shifting to the familiar "tu," he carried on:

"In security ... Yes, I work as a security guard! Haven't you noticed that you only ever see Blacks in dark suits standing in front of those perfume stores, in all the McDonald's and malls and God knows where else? Why don't Whites work security, you tell me? Anytime you see a White guy, he's there to tell you what to do! Either because he's the boss, or because he's the head of human resources. This means it's down to us to handle all those hoodlums, because those Whites bossing us around, they wet their pants at the slightest trouble! That's the Black man's destiny: to guard the White man and watch over his property, it's as simple as that!"

He stopped talking for a moment and checked his surroundings. The security guard's instincts, I thought to myself.

I started pedaling again. Instinctively he wiped his brow with his towel even though I was the one perspiring.

"Yes, my brother, mark my words, if I'm working security, it's because I don't want to come across as a complete failure. I've got my kids to think of, and all those car repair bills, the heating during the winter months, et cetera. How are we expected to make it? And then for all Africans of France, time isn't working in our favor, it keeps ticking away, and one day you get up and look in the mirror and realize you don't have a pension, and that you've been stuck paying rent for some crappy subsidized apartment while those twenty-something whiteys are already homeowners. That's why Whites are always in a hurry and checking their watches, whereas in Africa time is elastic, you can stretch it out as much as you like! That's our problem, we keep telling ourselves the 'time will come,' but it never does, never put off to tomorrow what you can do today, or as we used to say back in my village, from waiting around all day, the toad never had time to grow a tail! Yes, the Whites know that time is made of leather and that you can only pull at it so much before it tears and you end up with your destiny all in pieces. Let's be clear on this, my brother: the revolution must start with this. We need to take their time from them and give them ours if we don't want to end up like those tailless toads!"

His eyes betrayed a bitterness which over the years had turned into despair. He had decided to lance the boil:

"My brother, I'm telling you, my case is complicated, I'd even say a very special case! Guess where I work?"

He took a minute to catch his breath.

"I provide security at the headquarters of one of the country's two main political parties!"

"Which one? The PS or the UMP?"

"I'm not going to tell you which one because these walls have big ears that reach all the way to the Élysée Palace and I don't want to risk losing my little job that pays the bills and puts food on the table for my kids! And in any case, you're a writer and you might just repeat all this in your next book! Those Whites are too clever, they'll recognize me immediately ..."

"You're right," I murmured, just to say something.

"No, you don't get it, my brother, you're too disconnected, you're no longer a Negro like I am. You're still a Negro, but in a different category ..."

"You're wrong about that, my brother!"

"When it comes to me, I'm a Negro in Paris."

"And what does it mean to be a 'Negro in Paris'?"

"Just what it says, my brother! As far as I'm concerned, there's no difference between you and some White bourgeois guy. You can hang out with him and he won't be ashamed to tell other Whites you're his friend because it's very much in his interest to show others how he made you in his image. He'll even welcome you in his home, because at some point in time, when the White needs a Negro, he'll forget all about color. Color, my brother, is all about interest. If the White had to polish a Negro's shoes to hold on to his White privileges, he wouldn't think twice about doing it. But at the slightest false move or puffing up of his pectorals, that same White will remind you you're a good-for-nothing Negro. Yes, color is all about power and self-interest. What good could a guy like me possibly be to some White? What could I bring to him?"

Some White guy approached us at that precise moment. The dark-skinned brother suddenly stopped talking. Once the guy disappeared from view, he started up again:

"You see, they're everywhere! Do you think that White guy heard what we were saying?"

"I don't think so."

"Anyway, as I was saying, I work for one of the country's two main political parties. As it happens, we're a small group of Blacks who provide security for French politicians. Yes, for the same guys who write or vote on legislation aimed at chasing us out of the land. Do you think that's fair? Two of my colleagues even work for the far right. Do they have any choice in the matter? The hungry sheep will eat the first piece of grass that comes his way. My dream is to send my kids to the United States; at least they'll have their cushy lifestyles over there, especially with a Black president. That's certainly not about to happen over here any time soon!"

My workout was finally over. The brother kept following me. I could hear him in the shower stall next to me singing away in Sango, one of languages spoken in Central Africa.

We met up again in the locker rooms. I got dressed with my back to him, and when I turned around he was already wearing a dark blue suit with a white shirt.

"These are my work clothes, my brother ..."

I grabbed my gym bag. It seemed heavier, no doubt because I had just tossed my gear in haphazardly or perhaps because of the damp towel. I made my way to the stairs. The brother, who hadn't moved, practically yelled:

"Hey, mister writer, you've forgotten something!"

"What?"

He was beaming:

"Your cap!"

It was indeed lying there on the floor in front of the locker where I had gotten dressed. He picked it up and handed it to me. I was about to put it away in my bag when he firmly gripped my hand:

"No, my brother, I want you to put it on …"

I did what he asked, and we made our way down the stairs, with him shadowing me …

Once outside, the brother accompanied me as far as the metro entrance. We'd hardly spoken on the way there.

Before parting ways, he tapped me on the shoulder:

"Look out for yourself, my brother, the Blacks in this country are terrible! They have yet to understand that we need to work together like the fingers of our hand. Be careful, there'll be blows, because they don't think you deserve all that you have! No matter what, you can count on me …"

He handed me a piece of paper:

"He's my number. If you ever have a problem in this country, give me a call, I'm around French politicians all the time, I protect them, I know their mistresses and lovers, even the French don't get to see them as I do."

We said our goodbyes after a long handshake. He couldn't resist giving me a big hug.

"Keep speaking about us, my brother, and no matter what don't become one those smiling Banania Negroes like some of our brothers who shall remain nameless.[1] Those guys fight to pick up the crumbs the Whites leave for them and are willing to trade their souls for a bowl of beans …"

As I was about to step into the metro, he called after me:

"Hey, writer!"

I walked back toward him.

"I read something recently in Régis Debray's book *The Masks* that struck me. Do you know what he has to say about destiny?"

I shook my head.

"That's all I'm going to say. Get a copy of it and you'll see just how terrible destiny can be ..."

Since I didn't say anything, he felt the need to add:

"I know I've said too much ... I'm fairly sure you'll use what I've just said in one of your novels. But please don't use my real name. Speak instead of a dark-skinned brother you met who was from somewhere in Central Africa, but don't reveal my country's real name so that the Whites won't be able to recognize me ..."

No sooner than I had sat down in a carriage, I started scribbling down a few notes on our meeting, respecting, of course, my brother's last wishes not to mention, no matter what, the name of his country.

A Black guy was sitting opposite me on a fold-down seat. We just stared at each other. In the United States, there's always kind of a "little magic" that passes when Blacks meet, an acknowledgment of one another, a quick smile or the exchange of a 'Hi, Brother!'.

I smiled at him, but he didn't return my smile. Instead, he looked the other way, and then jumped off hurriedly when the train stopped at Croix de Chavaux ...

The next day, I went to the Gibert bookstore in the Latin Quarter and picked up a used copy of Debray's book. The pages had turned slightly yellow over time and there were a few grease marks on the cover. I wondered how many people must have browsed through it for it to be in this condition. In any case, it was the only copy left. I quickly flipped through the book: one reader had marked up a number of passages with a yellow fluorescent marker, but none had anything to do with destiny.

I made my way over to the nearby Luxembourg Gardens and found a nice quiet bench on which I could while away the time. From time to time I looked up to watch the procession of ducks and the children throwing them bits of bread.

I eventually found the passage the "Central African" was most likely referring to:

"Destiny is not some capricious old whore. But rather a conscientious civil servant, a deaf-mute wearing a tie who gets up every morning and rushes full-speed ahead to the office."[2]

3 The Spirit of the Laws

I'D LIKE TO say a few words about what is increasingly being referred to as "Black France," a term that might provide race demagogues and fundamentalists with proof of the existence of people of color in France. This is something I am convinced could threaten the very idea of a nation founded on a common destiny.[1]

Article 1 of the French Republic's constitution should, in theory at least, make any discussion impossible on the question of a "Black France" given that the Republic is "one and indivisible, secular, democratic and social" and that it "ensure[s] the equality of all citizens before the law, without distinction of origin, race or religion." But we all know that laws are one thing and reality quite another. France's constitution is so wonderful that it is unworkable. However, while we're on the subject, do we need to be reminded that a good number of countries, in particular former French colonies, blindly copied the document even though the regimes that have since claimed it are for the most part banana republics?

What is the true picture of France today? In clear and unequivocal terms, and whether one likes it or not, there is today a "Black presence" in France. Take a ride on the Paris metro, get off for a few minutes at the Château Rouge or Château d'Eau stops or visit some of the outer districts of large metropolitan areas—areas in which neighborhoods have been renamed "Mississippi" or "Bamako." For those of us who've come from elsewhere or who were born here of foreign parents and now have French nationality, these excursions should be enough to make us want to put away all our French history books. For these persons of color are full-fledged French citizens. In fact, it's the expression "average French person" that should probably be reformulated, because these men and women are the ones who've been busy writing and rewriting the pages of national history. The nation should instead try and find a way to accept and live with this newfound reality, especially if it wants to avoid the feeling of racial domination from spreading.

Europeans, Antilleans, Guyanese, Africans, Haitians, and Réunionese, together we have created from scratch an entirely new France. Having said this, and if indeed we have every right to denounce the injustices we have suffered, we must also question our own attitude which, at times, feeds gregarious instincts that are incompatible with the spirit of the nation. Africans themselves often conceive of France as a White country. Much in the same way that for some French people, to talk of France is to evoke a country made up of White people. Unlike the United States of America, France has not really accepted cohabitation between distinct "ethnic" groups, or, for that matter, been completely free to explore the "ethnic question" without such approaches causing a public outcry. Ethnic statistics or categories pertaining to one's origin shouldn't jeopardize the principle of belonging to the nation.[2] But in France, these kinds of practices are considered unconstitutional, and it is precisely this "unconstitutionality" that conceals injustices. Under the pretext of an allegedly collective equality, large segments of the French population find themselves sidelined from democracy.

The Black presence across the Atlantic can be explained, among other reasons, by the Triangular trade, but the same does not hold true when it comes to mainland France. We went through history as "savages" and "natives," later as African *tirailleurs* infantryman, before finally realizing what the White people really meant when they uttered the word *Negro*. The responsibility came down to us to distort the word, to transform it into something we could be proud of—much in the same way as African Americans had previously done—and we took hold of the term and in doing so launched the *Négritude* movement that remains to this day one of the most significant in Black thought. Négritude stood up in the face of a White world that had bestowed upon itself the right to impose its purportedly "enlightened" civilization on barbarians entangled in the forces of darkness and obscurantism. It is no exaggeration to say that from the very beginning it was Whites who invented Blacks, which meant that Blacks were compelled to define Whites according to their own vocabulary, often in a stereotypical manner given that the only image they had of them was the product of a tumultuous encounter defined by trickery, invasion, conquest, captivity, and domination.

What was so offensive about the words "Noir" or "Negro" for them to be later replaced by the anglophone term "Black"? Each era has its own vocabulary and way of watering down its concepts. Anglophones also used the term *Negro*, or worse even, *Nigger*. The fact remains that other expressions would also be used to refer to us, to question our presence and in the end its very legitimacy by lumping us as all together according to more generic terms: ultimately, we became, quite simply, *immigrants*, even when France was the only territory we'd ever known!

The presence of Blacks in France is the result of a long, convoluted history, the outcome of a multiplicity of factors which, among others, include the policies of the host country during some of its darkest periods, the search for a better life by Africans and populations from the overseas departments, or even the emergence of a generation that no longer has any ties with the African continent but who feel they have not been recognized in the country in which they were born.

In the minds of many, Blacks of France are considered as one large unified mass capable of speaking collectively and of impacting French politics. But this is nothing short of an illusion: the heterogeneous composition of this population has always led me to refute the idea that such a "community" exists. Beyond the color of their skin, what does a Black person with legal papers studying at Sciences Po possibly have in common with a Haitian refugee or a Black Antillean from one of the overseas departments that is fully integrated to French territory? Absolutely nothing. For the most part, they don't even know one another and their relations are essentially based on the prejudices of Western societies, the same kind that served to justify slavery or colonialism. In France, the Senegalese, Réunionese, and Congolese are strangers to one another, not speaking a common language originating in Africa but rather French. Proud of being Black sisters and brothers, proud of hailing from the "cradle of humanity," the only possible basis for establishing a link would be the history of slavery or colonization, even though most societies have some kind of experience of domination. Do we even need to remind ourselves of those Blacks who enslaved other Blacks? For slavery to provide the bond for a community in France would require that the majority of Blacks who ended up on this territory did so as a result of this particular trade. That's where the argument doesn't hold, and this explains the fascination with the African American experience, almost as if these "sisters" and "brothers" were to be envied for being snatched from the Black continent. However, unlike the Blacks of France, those folks don't have a "fallback territory" they can turn to. Today, when African Americans experience injustice, they can hardly say: "If you don't want me here, then I'll go back to my country of origin." But in France, some Blacks can *still* say that, or at the very least, point to their parents' country of origin, that "mythical territory" of the ancestors. But are these countries of substitution not also impediments to the emergence of another France? In sum, a good number of Blacks in France are, to some extent, *citizens of the alternative*. The logic goes something like this: *If I am not accepted here, I can always go over there, prepared to lose myself even more in my country of origin or at least that of my parents.*

Today, it is nothing short of outright heresy to say out loud that one is no longer from over there but rather definitively from here. In the eyes of many French people, we remain "French by interest" and, if that is indeed the case, then a people who desperately want to be admitted to a territory while at the same time clinging in their unconscious—and even their consciousness—to a substitute territory, a mythic territory which, in reality, is not waiting for them. When they do travel there, they are seen as tourists, as people who have come from the North. When it comes down to it, the ones that actually choose to settle there are few and far between.

The question is not therefore whether to erase one's origins, for that would be to go against a constitution that "ensure[s] the equality of all citizens before the law, without distinction of origin, race or religion." Instead, and this is the real challenge, how can one best identify those elements from our different "belongings" that could help build a sense of a common destiny. In other words, as Amin Maalouf has underscored, "everyone should be able to include in what he regards as his own identity a new ingredient, one that will assume more and more importance in the course of the new century and the new millennium: the sense of belonging to the human adventure as well as to his own."[3]

4 Murderous Identities

You have to be on your guard when you enter an airport, for you may very well discover your *identity* there or, much to your astonishment, be assigned a new one.

On one such occasion, I was getting ready to catch Air France flight number 0067 in Los Angeles. I had just presented my passport to the American agent when a man came up to me. I recognized him immediately: I'd spotted him earlier in the check-in line, dressed in all-white linen clothing, and grinning at me each time our eyes met.

He was tall and thin, exceptionally tanned, with hair down to his shoulders. Staring fixedly at my passport, he asked:

"Are you French?"

Defiantly, I responded:

"Isn't it obvious?"

He smiled again, let me know that he had been living in California for a while, that he was from Normandy and on his way to his aunt's funeral in Caen. I offered my condolences. Despondent, he sighed:

"In any case, she'd already suffered so much that death was a relief..."

Then he was suddenly all smiles again and asked me if I'd read a book he hastened to retrieve from his satchel. *The Map and the Territory* by Michel Houellebecq.[1] No, I hadn't read it.

"You have to read it, it's a great book!"

I was pretty sure he wasn't interested in talking to me about literature and that he had something else on his mind.

As we were heading for the gate, he finally jumped right in and asked:

"Your parents ... *I mean*, your father and your mother, where do they come from?"

I knew this question was coming, although I was surprised it had taken him so long to ask it. Usually people just come straight out with it: when a White and a Black French person first meet, the former invariably inquires, in their own convoluted way, as to the "real origins" of the latter.

And so, to rattle this indiscreet compatriot, I decided to spice things up a little:

"My parents are French."

He looked at me as if I was some kind of rare species. Not giving up, he went on:

"So, if I understand correctly then, you were adopted by a French family?"

"No."

Now he really didn't know what to say next. From the look in his eyes, he seemed to be imploring me to confess. What a strange Frenchmen I was, capable in one easy gesture of undermining all the certainties he'd collected in various history textbooks. How was I supposed to explain to him in a few words how my mother and my father—born prior to independence—had remained French "without even being aware of it"? In fact, they would have had to actually *renounce* their French citizenship after the emancipation of the Congo. Not surprisingly, progenitors had other things on their mind at the time than this administrative step, the consequences of which they failed to measure at the time. Independence itself was a rather vague notion to them. Whites were still to be seen in the streets of our cities, and nothing had really changed. My father still worked for the Whites in a hotel in the city center and my mother sold peanuts in Pointe-Noire's market, far from all the grand debates initiated by the former colonizer and by the Blacks who would henceforth govern us. Many Africans of their generation found themselves in the exact same circumstances and were therefore French without even being aware of it, especially if they didn't know how to read and write.

When I was studying law in Nantes—before they tightened the naturalization laws—descendants of the formerly colonized could demand the "recovery of nationality" from their parents. Indeed, I'd told several Africans about this possibility as they rushed over to the municipal registry offices to request original copies of their birth certificates in order to initiate the naturalization process. Some of these Africans were so incredulous they took me for some lunatic. But the legislative texts were quite clear on this, and France had no other option but to administer the laws it had voted in. One can just imagine the look on the faces of the registrars down at the municipal offices in Nantes, suddenly overwhelmed by the avalanche of requests. The word was on the street and now all the Africans wanted to recover their parents' nationality and become full-fledged citizens. And so by the time the offices opened, they were already lined up at the counter, stating boldly:

"I'm French and I didn't know it!"

I wasn't about to launch into a lengthy discussion on legislation right here in the Tom Bradley International Terminal at Los Angeles Airport. A wall stood between me and this guy from Normandy. We were the embodiment of two types of French people. He adhered to a very strict interpretation of nationality, one restricted to natural-norn citizens who also happened to be natural-born to White French parents, whereas for me, French citizenship was something that originated in one's soul and conscience and that implied a degree of commitment.

And so, without actually revealing my country of origin—which he desperately wanted to know—I explained to him that while he was *born* French, I had *become* French.

Now he was more confused than ever, and suggested we go grab a cup of coffee at Starbucks. Of course, he seized the opportunity to tout the "real coffee" from France, that also happened to be the best in the world, especially when compared to the kind served in America that smelled like wild cat urine. He put his Houellebecq novel back in his satchel:

"I'll get back to it on the plane. I'm almost half way through it ..."

We still had an hour to kill before boarding. He mentioned his aunt again, who'd been ailing in hospital. I half-listened to him, distracted as I was by his summery clothes. I imagined him leading a life of luxury, punctuated by nocturnal forays on Malibu's beaches, romanticized around the world by the TV series *Baywatch*. In fact, our friend from Normandy could easily have been cast in the series.

His outfit perfectly matched his somewhat unusual phrasing, and I was amazed by the degree to which he struggled to express himself in French. His sentences were peppered with American words, and from time to time I had to jump in with the correct French word, while he rolled his eyes and muttered:

"How do you say that again in French, I've been *upgraded*, I'm in *business* and ..."

"You have been 'surclassé.'"

"'Surclassé!' *Yes, that's the fucking word!* Tell me, how do you hold on to your French? How long have you been in the States?"

"Eight years …"

"Holy shit! I can't believe that! You're kidding me! I've been here five years and I've almost forgotten it completely, *you know!"*

As we made our way over to the gate, he threw out one more question:

"You know, between us, I know guys who are Franco-Cameroonian, others who are Franco-Senegalese, *I mean,* you've gotta be Franco-something, right?"

I didn't respond. The Franco-Norman made his way into the business class section, and I didn't run into him again while I was waiting at baggage claim in Paris.

No sooner had I sat down on the plane than I opened my Moleskine notebook and wrote down the expression "Franco-something." This fellow countryman wasn't completely wrong. Many French people have trouble accepting that some of their compatriots don't look like them and that the idea of a White France has become an illusion, a frozen image condemning all those who acquired French nationality to devoting their lives to justifying, explaining their origins to citizens of "pure stock," almost having to apologize for holding a French passport. But was it up to me or him to apologize?

At the risk of disappointing our "Franco-Norman," I would say that I'm more of a "Congo-something," only too aware of the fact that I was born elsewhere. My understanding of *identity* goes far beyond notions of *territory* or *blood.* Each new encounter nourishes me, including the one I'd just had with the "Franco-Norman." Limiting oneself to a single territory would be futile, to ignore all the ways in which the world has become increasingly interconnected and, over and above that, to take into account the complexity of this new era that binds us to each other far beyond geographic considerations.

The history of colonization has taught us that a territory can just as well be imaginary, exist beyond borders, brave environmental factors, or mix languages and races. To that end, didn't France expand overseas by building an empire whose power and influence once shined in the eyes of the world? In 1966, during a visit to the island of Martinique, General de Gaulle famously exclaimed before the native population: "My God how French you are!"

In those days, the nation was perceived in a broader sense—even from an ideological standpoint. It was founded on the objective of bolstering its position in the world. Even today, France is still made up of all its overseas departments and territories, a fact that should be sufficient to reframe the way in which we conceive of territory, unless, of course, one thinks of these islands merely as spots for pale-skinned folks from the mainland to go and work on their tans. As the seventeenth-century playwright Corneille once wrote, "Rome is no longer just in Rome, it is there wherever I am," thereby dispelling the very idea of a fixed territory. And as for the French capital itself, let's not forget that it too was once "displaced" during the German Occupation. Paris was no longer just in Paris, and Brazzaville was suddenly thrust into the new role as the capital of Free France, while at the same time, Radio-Brazzaville became the "voice of France." The historian Olivier Luciani summarized the situation as follows: "On the one hand, since the summer of 1940, Free France has imposed on its colonies particularly heavy demands in terms of war efforts. On the other, President Roosevelt has made no secret of his desire to replace the colonial empire with an international system of trusteeship."[2] In the words of Charles de Gaulle in his *Memoirs*, France had to fight to hold on to its "possessions." It was in this same capital that the famous Brazzaville Conference was held in 1944, gathering "the senior colonial officials in the presence of Charles de Gaulle, in order to prepare reforms that could be implemented after the liberation of France. The goal was to undertake modest renovations to the colonial empire while still maintaining it."[3]

Why do we always have to wait for a major disaster or another global conflict to demystify the notion of territory? No matter what, we will have achieved something of value once we finally recognize that each and every French person brings in their "wake" a piece of the national territory everywhere they go, that they are accountable for its reputation, even ultimately for its depreciation abroad. When a person of color commits a crime and speaks in French on American television, people point the finger at France and never at the culprit's country of origin. In truth, France takes credit for the achievements of its nationals of color abroad.

Before he became a singer, the example of Yannick Noah had become an old joke. Whenever he was knocked out of a big tournament, the French media referred to him as "Franco-Cameroonian," but when he won the French Open at Roland-Garros in 1983, people rejoiced in the victory of the great "French tennis player." Can Jo-Wilfried Tsonga, currently one of the top players in the world and whose father is Congolese from Brazzaville, expect the same fate?

By contrast, in America, I regularly run into French people who *truly* consider me to be one of their compatriots, which always leaves me with the impression that once abroad, whatever their racial background happens to be, the French broaden their perception of citizenship. Almost as if, so as to better define what a nation is, we should all leave the territory and meet up some place in which our culture would emerge as the only substantial link.

I often wander up and down Third Street Promenade, the busiest tourist thoroughfare in Santa Monica, lined with luxury shops, bustling with all kinds of attractions and street musicians trying their best to grab the attention of the passersby. A bit further on, where Colorado Boulevard ends, the famous Santa Monica Pier, with all its rides and restaurants, juts out into the Pacific Ocean. It's a must-stop for someone arriving from France, unless, of course, they'd rather sit in traffic around the downtown Los Angeles area than enjoy the splendor of Santa Monica beach. I can always spot a French person a mile off. They move around in groups, occasionally raising their voice to comment on some American whose obesity they find shocking, while the person in question quietly goes about their business, completely unaware. And so I wasn't the slightest bit surprised when, on one of my walks, I overheard ignominious mockery in the language of Voltaire, so to speak:

"Check out that fatso? How much do you have to eat to look that? He could at least cover up his fat rolls? Honestly, those Americans!"

I couldn't help myself laughing in the face of such impudence. They all turned around at once, and the oldest in the gang sighed:

"Ah, finally, a French person!"

After a few words, I insinuated ironically that most of the obese Americans in Santa Monica spoke perfect French. They snickered. The guy asked me what I was doing in this city and whether, like them, I too was on vacation. I nodded, without elaborating. In the end we all sat down at a Mexican restaurant on the corner of Second Street and Wilshire, and in no time our conversation turned to French politics. As the old French guy pointed out, we were behaving like "real French people," which means that we were expressing our opinions of the current government, of Parisians, on the discrepancy between the numbers reported by the police and those of the trade unions during strikes, on minimum welfare benefits, and all the rotten TV shows. I never once got the impression that they thought of me as a foreigner. If anything, I was more of a safety net for them, able to understand what they were saying, because I was one of them. The youngest among them, his face covered in acne, was moving to Venice, a neighborhood adjacent to Santa Monica. His father was really proud of his progeny who would soon be attending my university. As we said our farewells, he made a point of saying to him:

"You're lucky, Bernard, you know, to have met a fellow Frenchman. It's important having a mentor in a city you don't know …"

Meeting French tourists is one thing, but one should not forget the reality that there are more and more citizens susceptible to a rhetoric designed to play on people's fears of the other and who believe that the territory needs to be defended in order to safeguard their identity. They have in their sights international conventions that have provisions for the circulation of goods and people, notably the Schengen Agreement, in which the signatory states to the agreement have abolished all internal borders. But what would the "French genius" be without confrontation with other spaces? In some cases, ideas were perfected or improved thanks to the influences that came, precisely because of migrants, from outside of the territory of origin and which, through contact with other cultures, helped redefine the analyses of "nationals" and resulted in significant, at times even sweeping changes. How, for example, can one begin to explain the revolution that occurred in "Black world" thought sprouted outside of the African continent, initiated in the diaspora? The Négritude movement—launched by Léopold Sédar Senghor, Aimé Césaire, and Léon-Gontran Damas—was born in France and after years of exchanges with the African American writers of the *Harlem Renaissance* living in exile in France because of racial segregation in their country. Back in those days, France became their "imaginary homeland," a land of hospitality for the persecuted.

If the notion of territory needs to be reconsidered, then the same holds true when it comes to so-called "national" identity. But, no doubt, it would also be necessary to return to the origins of this concept and see how far those who traffic in fear have been willing to go so as to transform a dynamic concept into a static and suicidal ideology. Do dictionaries have any say in the matter? "Identity" comes from the Vulgar Latin *identitas*, which means "that which is the same," a word that is itself derived from the Latin *idem*. At the time, identity described "similitude," and then later, "that which is one." The *Dictionnaire historique de la langue française* specifies that both existing law and common usage defined the word in such a manner that it "made provisions for somebody to be an individual and to be recognized as such."[4] In other words, the core of identity is first and foremost attached to the self, to the ego, to the existence of an individual within a society. It's what defines the uniqueness of the individual or the group. Just as an individual has an identity card, so too does the group. But then, one may well ask, what elements would actually make up the group's identity card? How would these various elements be chosen? Without measuring the extent of contemporary society's transformation, and therefore neglecting in this supposed *national identity* the true face of France, some have dreamed up an *ad hoc* ministry with the aim of misleading people into believing that social behavior can be governed by decree. Taking advantage of this breach, these same people have resorted to a range of archaic arguments and abstract values in order to poach far-right voters. Who in France today would be capable of defining national identity? If you listen to those who promote it, you might be led to believe that we were facing a serious "identity crisis" that could somehow stymie France's progress!

In this respect, what is needed, to paraphrase the title of a book by the sociologist Jean-Claude Kaufmann, is for us to instigate "an invention of the self."[5] In effect, Kaufmann "offers every individual the recognition, approval, and the love of others necessary in order to feel like a full-fledged individual."[6] The individual only truly exists when recognition is bestowed by the group, all the more so since it is the law of the given group that determines the procedures for individual mobility. Pockets of resistance have cropped up here and there due to lack of recognition from the Republic. Various groups have come up with their own laws and targeted those who have never set foot in those underprivileged "zones" or neighborhoods, yet who don't hesitate to point the finger from the safety and comfort of their elite fortresses. Autonomous identities have sprung up in these urban areas, rejecting collective norms that always leave the impression of being more implacable with those who consider themselves the pariahs of the Republic.

The debates launched in France on national identity back during the 2000s were not enough to temper the multiple crises of the "self." At the end of the day, what is this national identity people speak of? At the highest levels of the State, even President Sarkozy couldn't make heads or tails of it, content with repeating during his presidential campaign that it consisted in "saying who we are." But what about what we may become?

For journalists Cordélia Bonal and Laure Équy, writing in a column published in *Libération* newspaper, national identity is "above all an electoral catch-word, a prominent talking point which—along with the idea of 'work value'—candidate Sarkozy repeated during his 2007 campaign."[7] As a rule, filler stories during electoral campaigns are usually content with simply distracting or misleading people, with selling sand in the desert or shampoo to the bald. Demagogy based on a group's identity cohesion is our politician's latest discovery.

Let's be very clear on this. National identity is above all the French themselves. But what exactly would the composite drawing of a French person look like today? I wouldn't dare ask my "Franco-Norman" compatriot, because his response would surely be devastating ...

5 Road to Europe

WILL EUROPEANS EVER really fully be able to understand what goes on inside the mind of an African kid as he imagines this continent to the north, convinced it's the place where dreams come true? I was one of those children who took pleasure daydreaming in this way, but I eventually came to see how it had all been a sham.

My father used to say, his index finger pointing to the horizon, that Europe was all that lay beyond the ocean. Growing up in Pointe-Noire, we held on to that conviction. Only much later—when I was actually living in France—did I realize that, as naive an explanation as his may very well have been, my father had in fact been way ahead of his time. Although he passed away a while ago, his deep and reassuring voice often came back to me. Europe was in fact an idea, a belief, a conviction. Everyone was free to invent it as they saw fit. To accede to it, all you had to do was believe. But isn't *accession* a term that is often used when talking about the European Union? What's a human enterprise worth that's not based on a common, shared idea?

As we ran along the Côte Sauvage until we were out of breath, under the gaze of the Beninese fishermen, we used to shout out:

"We're going to *go to Europe!*"

Most of the ships anchoring in the port of Pointe-Noire came from that distant continent. We envied the proud cormorants and the august albatrosses that accompanied them. Europe was embodied in the sailors who came ashore and took the city by storm, hanging out in the bars in the Quartier Trois-Cents neighborhood, their muscles stamped with tattoos, more often than not fire-breathing dragons.

We'd read all the extraordinary stories about the freebooters. Were we trying to look like them when we wore earrings or attempted to copy their tattoos on our still-frail muscles? Tu us, all these black, yellow, or red sailors were all "people from Europe." Because of the ocean, everything that "emerged" from the sea could only have come from there.

There were maps all over the classroom walls at the Trois-Glorieuses school, but we couldn't care less about the mathematical equations with multiple unknown variables, the drawing of a digestive tract, or the longitudinal cross-section of a molar. The only one that mattered was the map of Europe …

Mr. Dupré, who'd left his snow-covered continent several decades previously, with a keen eye, suntanned skin, pointed his ruler toward his native Poitou-Charentes region. It was thanks to him that we learned Europe was not a single country, that it was not unified linguistically or ethnically, as we'd initially thought, but also that it was dominated by Christianity. Our avid eyes were glued to the map, and scrutinized the smallest detail, followed the waterways and the turbulent rivers. Nevertheless, a hint of chauvinism prevailed and we couldn't help but finding our own geography all the more impressive. The map of Europe was quite different from that of Africa, made up as it was of intertwined foreign lands with chaotic, hazardous borders. Spain glanced at Morocco toward the city of Tangiers; France plunged its pointed nose into the Atlantic Ocean, but found herself almost smothered by England, perched as it was atop her head; Italy reminded us, of course, of the narrow stiletto heels the ladies of the night wore over in the Rex quarter; Norway, Sweden, and Finland looked like a tightly curled up centipede tickling Denmark.

The geography lessons were one thing, but the names of several European cities became forever engraved in our memories in Mrs. Paraiso's history classes: Berlin, Helsinki, Danzig, Warsaw, Nuremberg, Sarajevo, Vienna …

We dreamed of Europe, of this elegant and distinguished woman, adorned with jewels, her arms outstretched to us whenever we approached the shoreline. But with time we lost hope of Europe ever coming to us, of rising from the waves. The hours we whiled away on the shore seemed endless.

We now had to look to the skies above: that airplane piercing the clouds could only have been heading to Europe. Anywhere but Libreville, or worse even, Bangui or Douala! To get to those places, there was grandfather's pirogue, or even the magic carpet of some local charlatan whose favorite bedside books included *The Thousand and One Nights* or *One Hundred Years of Solitude* …

My father met many Europeans at the Victory Palace Hotel where he worked. One day, he came home with a piece of fruit in his hand.

"What do you call this fruit?" he asked.

I kept my eye on the fruit but remained silent.

"It's an apple," I eventually said.

"That's true, it is an apple, but it is also Europe … This fruit comes from a long way away, smell it …"

I slowly brought it up to my nose as my father kept repeating:

"This perfume, that's Europe!"

My view of this continent has not changed. I'm still very much attached to these simple, understated, efficient images, and among them that of the apple my father once held in his hand.

Nevertheless, there was also a degree of confusion when it came to our perception of Europe. For the Congolese, Europe is above all associated with the arrival of the first Whites in the fifteenth century: the Portuguese. One of their chiefs, Diogo Cão, was looking for a way to connect the Atlantic and Indian Oceans. He was also searching for the Christian realm of Prester John. However, since the ways of God are inscrutable, he went astray and happened upon the Kongo kingdom. That's when our ancestors saw a White person for the first time and these Portuguese had come by sea! So, my father was right when it came to the Atlantic Ocean …

Only, try and pronounce the word "Portuguese"! It was easier for us to say the *Mputuguezos*. To us, a White foreigner who arrived from the sea could only be a *Mputuguezo*. The word *Mputu* was synonymous with Europe and going to Europe meant going to *Mputu*. We dreamed of a vast, endless territory. My aunt, who hadn't been to school and who suffered from elephantiasis, murmured some time before she passed:

"I'm no fool, I know I'm going to die. But those who die will always be resurrected: they'll be resurrected in *Mputu*, behind the ocean …"

When we urged her to tell us what Europe was like, she answered pointing down at her feet:

"People over there all live in the water. That's why their feet don't hurt like mine do!"

My aunt took her idea of Europe with her to the grave …

Deep down inside, each child from the African continent draws this distant land where snow falls. A land of opportunity and happiness, a dream that is most likely the source of all the blind fascination that drives African migrants on tragic adventures. The road to Europe thus becomes a Way of the Cross. One will recall the two Guinean adolescents, Yaguine Koïta and Fodé Tounkara, both fourteen years old, stowaways on a Sabena Airlines flight from Conakry to Brussels. Their bodies were discovered on August 2, 1999, in the landing gear of the airplane at Brussels International Airport. Plastic bags were recovered from their belongings containing their civil documents and school report cards, along with a "will" prepared by the boys and addressed to "Excellencies, Messrs. members and officials of Europe," the concluding words of which moved people the world over: "Therefore, if you see that we have sacrificed ourselves and risked our lives, this is because we suffer too much in Africa and that we need you to fight against poverty and to put an end to the war in Africa …"[1]

The road to Europe leaves young Africans with the impression that the adventure will end in a clearing from which misery will have finally disappeared thanks to a magic wave of the wand. In the Congo, this dream culture is sustained by those who have already crossed the Rubicon. These folks are called the "Parisians." For them, going to France is not that different from making the pilgrimage to Mecca. The "Parisians," preoccupied with their clothing as members of the SAPE movement, deliberately neglect to talk to their young compatriots back home about the other face of Europe, with its high unemployment, its homeless problem, the delicate economic situation as well as the xenophobic rhetoric associated with certain political parties and that has become so prevalent as to be banal.[2]

Yet, listening to these "Parisians," one could easily come away believing that anything was possible in Europe, and that getting there should be everyone's goal. The vast majority of these "Parisians" had made it to Paris or Brussels following an "adventure," one that had invariably began in Angola before the onward journey to Europe via Portugal.

In addition, the road to Europe has also fed the artist's imagination as well as several writers from the Black continent, most notably from the 1990s on, including novels such as *L'impasse* or *Le paradis du nord*, works that are indicative of Africa's entry into a period of what has become known as "Afropessimism," and that was the outcome of long-standing dictatorships.[3] These novels are like alarm bells. They feature marginal characters trapped on the Black continent and mired in their illusions, and who, for the most part, end up at an "impasse." Yet how many young Africans wouldn't push these books aside while insisting that the road to Europe still holds promise:

"Whatever, they're only novels! The real truth comes from the mouth of the 'Parisians'! If it's the last thing I do, I'll make it to Europe!"

6   How Can One Be Persian?

Since the 1990s, immigration in France has been two and a half times lower than in other European countries.[1] Furthermore, the majority of immigrants in France are from other European countries rather than from other continents. No politician would dare say that though, out of fear of losing voters to the far right that, as the socialist Laurent Fabius once famously said as prime minister back in 1984, "asks the right questions" but gives the "wrong answers." Among these "right questions," immigration features prominently. The more interesting thing to note on this subject is that virtually all of the French political class, following Fabius, concur on the issue.

Immigrants have found themselves at the center of some of the most heated debates the country has seen. The immigrant was considered an alien at the time of the Vichy regime, but after World War II, France encouraged immigration and family reunification. The focus at the time was on economic recovery. Thereafter, especially from the 1960s on, the constant back and forth on policy meant that the status of the immigrant was hard to pin down. Hostels were set up to "park" the hordes of immigrants that had come from elsewhere, but at the same time, efforts were also being made to restrict new arrivals. During Valéry Giscard d'Estaing's presidency (1974–1981), immigrants who had settled in France were offered lump sum payments to encourage them to leave. When the Socialists came to power in 1981, the prime minister talked about immigration in terms of "the weight of the world." These words have resonated down through the intervening years and are worth citing in their entirety since they are often taken out of context: "This is why I believe that we cannot welcome the weight of the world, that France must remain true to itself, a land of political asylum—we are signatories of the Geneva Convention which provides conditions for receiving all those whose freedom of opinion and expression has been restricted—but no more."

François Mitterrand's presidency (1981–1995) saw the first charter flights commissioned to send immigrants back to their country of origin. Later, Jacques Chirac spoke of the "noise and the smell." Neither the left nor the right could ever claim ownership over the issue, and very early on immigration was instrumentalized for electoral gain by preying on people's deep-seated fears of foreigners. It would be a grave error to blame all of this exclusively on the National Front. So much so that those who today point the finger at immigrants—or, let's not beat about the bush, at "Arabs and Blacks"—have become "heroes," wallowing like martyrs who are being prevented from speaking out. Éric Zemmour and Robert Ménard can be counted among such "heroes." The former, seen as a kind of "maverick,"[2] asked on a television show: "Why are police stops so frequent? Why is that? Because most of the drug dealers are Blacks or Arabs, that's how it is, it's a fact."[3] Several judgments have been delivered against him for incitement to racial hatred. The media visibility of these individuals relies entirely on excess and provocation, and just by listening to them we become complicit.

As for Robert Ménard, the former secretary-general of the international NGO Reporters Without Borders, he used to be a journalist whose independent, iconoclastic, and committed positions I once respected, at least until he came out in support of Marine Le Pen National Front in the 2011 regional elections. Interviewed on RTL radio, he was adamant: "It's not so much that I understand them, but rather that I agree with them."[4] He also coauthored (with Emmanuelle Duverger) a short pamphlet entitled *Vive Le Pen!* for the sole purpose of expressing his "indignation" at those who were demonizing the far-right electorate, especially in the media, and who, according to the pamphleteers, were throwing their weight around before the National Front.[5] The authors were careful to specify that they were not defending either the father or the daughter Le Pen but rather denouncing "the witch-hunt" and the haste with which the party's ideas were being discredited. Why should we not worry, along with Marie Guichoux, that such an ambiguous position "runs the risk of captivating National Front followers"?[6]

When I look at a map of France, every place is familiar to me. Yet, there's something about this map which is less appealing to me. It appears far from reality. I know deep down that this is not the France that had so fascinated me growing up in Africa. This is not the France I imagined from the streets of Pointe-Noire throughout my adolescence. This is not the France I found in the books I read. I dreamed of another

France, the one I'm still waiting for. The map of France I have before me is "white," an image we've been sold for decades now. A one-dimensional and *uniform* society. This uniformity soothes one's conscience, reassures those who yearn for a *certain* vision of this country. According to this *certain* idea, France's decline is the fault of the other. This same other that only appears on the evening news when a societal norm has been transgressed, or in stories featuring insalubrious environments to which primitive mores and wild animals have been imported.

For proponents of this uniformity, multiplicity—others might even say *diversity*—is perceived as an octopus threatening to engulf the "identity" that their Gallic ancestors bequeathed to them—those that had, as the poet Rimbaud once wrote in *A Season in Hell*, "the whitish blue eye, the narrow skull, and the awkwardness in combat." Not surprisingly, debates on these questions have centered on blood and soil, the original principles of nationality, along with other factors such as marriage, adoption, et cetera. Admittedly, France does, today at least, grant nationality to anyone born in French territory, whatever their origin may be. Nonetheless, and unlike Great Britain, Portugal, or Italy—and even Germany since 2000—this right remains conditional in France, and individuals must petition in the year after they turn eighteen. The Guigou Law of 1998 added the condition that the child have lived continuously or intermittently on French soil for at least five years. We are far from the spirit of the Constitution of 1791 that automatically provided citizenship to the children of foreigners born and living in France, and that the Civil Code would abrogate thirteen years later by reinstituting the primacy of blood ties. Citizenship based on the right of soil would only be reintroduced as a response to labor shortages and once the nation found itself again embroiled in military conflict. Granting nationality was a way for the nation to acknowledge all those contributing to its power and economic well-being. That the question remained a key political issue was understandable, and the reticence when it came to the right of soil stemmed from the perception that it would open up the country to family reunification and to a massive influx of immigrants. The way in which one acquires nationality thus ended up becoming an instrument for controlling migratory flows.

In contrast, *blood* became the preferred line of defense for inward-looking nations, the core argument for extremists calling for the preservation of "national identity." Blood made it possible for someone to qualify as "one hundred percent French," as if nationality was a question of percentages or of hemoglobin. Defining someone through blood, of course, means privileging a naturalist vision rather than a humanist approach that would be closer to the situation in present-day societies in which identity is the product of cultural diversity. In short, there are two categories of French people: those who have done nothing to be French and those who have had to perform the twelve labors of Hercules. The former consider themselves to be *naturally* French. Whereas for the latter, their belonging to the nation is permanently put into question, and once in a while the laws will even render them stateless. They may very well be French on paper, but the looks on people's faces continue to put into question their origins. How can one be Persian?

7 The Foreign Student

I ARRIVED IN France in the late 1980s to study law, thanks to a scholarship from the Congolese government. In those days, students like myself feared being sent to the Soviet Union. In the first place, because studying there was considered too "easy," and returnees were looked down upon, in contrast with those lucky enough to have gone to France and upon whom admiration was bestowed. Second, because the Communist ideology that was fashionable in our part of the world at the time had ended up repelling us, and the last thing we wanted was to end up in a country that had, in our eyes, replaced the former colonial powers. Our leaders sought inspiration from the Soviet model and went so far as to develop a cult of personality emblematic of that country. Portraits of our president lined the walls of the big city streets, and we were forced to commit his speeches to memory. Pupils and students were expected to join the Parti Congolais du Travail (PCT). We learned Russian beginning in secondary school, and they convinced us it would be the language of the "future," that people the world over would communicate in Russian in the decades to come. We despised English at the time, and if we held on to some esteem for French this was because it was not easy for the government to convince us that France was somehow decadent, and that Hugo, Lamartine, Proust, Zola, and Verne had suddenly become worthless. It would take a very clever person indeed to turn us off of these writers given that even the great Russian ones had nothing but deep respect for French literature. France therefore enjoyed a status apart, the only country spared from our desire to do battle with the values of capitalism.

As we observed the look of distress on the face of the Congolese students returning from the USSR and the way in which they were totally disconnected from reality, the Russian language gradually became as detestable to us as English was. One of the main differences between the Congolese who came back from France was evident in the status of their foreign wives. The Russian ones behaved just like their Congolese counterparts: they went to fetch water, prepared meals outside in a pot perched on three stones and heated with charcoal purchased at the end of the street; they also carried their offspring on their backs wrapped in a loincloth. As for the French women, they commanded a higher level of prestige and lived with their husbands in the city center. Visits with the couple were by appointment only. We should have given due credit to the Russian women for at least making the effort to fit in with Congolese culture, but we didn't. In our minds, the Whites should remain in their proper place and not give it up to local "barbarism." Some Congolese even felt ashamed for the Russian wives and would scurry over to their husbands to remind them of this:

"Really! Honestly! Are you forgetting she's White? How can you watch her humiliate herself in this way? Shame on you!"

Conversely, the French wives often came under attack. They were reproached for their colonial attitudes and for keeping their Congolese husband away from his friends. Nevertheless, our compatriots who married French women left us with the distinct impression they'd attained true civilization, whereas those who'd come back from the Soviet Union were still living in a ghetto. Moreover, the Soviet university that awarded the degrees was named after Patrice Lumumba! How could that possibly rival the Sorbonne?

No effort was therefore spared in trying to avoid being sent to the Soviet Union, and I therefore felt incredibly fortunate when I learned I'd been selected to leave for France, escaping the Communist brainwashing in the process . . .

I didn't study at the Sorbonne, but instead at the law school in Nantes. The Sorbonne? Everyone spoke of it as if it were some kind of temple to education, a place where one could rub shoulders with the next generation of French intellectuals. We were aware of the student demonstrations that had taken place there in May 1968 and of the forceful intervention by the police within the walls of the hallowed institution. These clashes reminded us of our own circumstances when, to voice our anger at our government for failing to pay our scholarships for months, we seized the most rudimentary weapons we could get our hands on when confronted by the Congolese police, who were armed to the teeth. If truth be told, it wasn't only the Sorbonne's prestige we were drawn to, but also the rebellious spirit of its students who appeared as hot-blooded as we were.

The university's reputation was so great in francophone sub-Saharan Africa that, in some capitals such as Abidjan, a number of the public spaces had been baptized "the Sorbonne." Lively exchanges took place there between doctoral students, unemployed graduates recently returned from France, or simply young people who aspired to enter politics but whose ambitions had thus far been hampered by the old-timers unwilling to give up their spots to the younger generation.

We also knew that the Sorbonne wasn't far from the Pantheon, the monument in which France paid homage to great men. It was therefore preferable to be a fool with a degree from the Sorbonne than a genius out of the University Patrice Lumumba who would end up as some kind of dignitary working for the PCT. Perhaps this was one of the aftereffects of colonization. In any event, France had done everything possible to ensure that we continued, even after independence, to identify with its educational system.

I will never forget my first day at law school in Nantes. Roger Le Moal, professor of private international law, had reached the point in his course in which he discussed the "status of foreigners in France." On that day, when I pushed open the door to the auditorium, I almost turned around instantly: I found myself standing in front of over three hundred attentive students, all of whom started to whisper once they spotted me. Instead of using one of the rear entrances, I'd inadvertently entered through the door reserved for the faculty. Caught off-guard, Roger Le Moal glanced at me and with a short jerk of the head, indicated where I should sit. I quickly scanned the room: I spotted three Blacks drowned in a sea of Whites, bunched together as if they were afraid the Europeans might devour them raw. These were fellow countrymen that had come ahead of me. The government had delayed purchasing my airline ticket and I'd only been able to leave two months after them. The last to arrive, I was still wearing summer clothes even though it was now the middle of winter. I couldn't have picked a better time to join the class, since the topic was of immediate concern to me. The professor was explaining, among other things, the process of recovering French nationality and how this applied to individuals whose parents had not renounced it after independence. These people could now legitimately recover French nationality by decree. I was therefore virtually French since my parents were in that category. I almost gasped in surprise, and asked myself how on earth all the foreigners from francophone sub-Saharan Africa living in France without papers were not aware of this legal loophole.

I had to make up for the two months I'd missed out of the school year. A French friend, Marie-Paule, helped me out by letting me borrow her class notes. She also showed me around Nantes, as well as the town of Noirmoutier where her family was from. Everywhere we went she introduced me as a "Congolese poet" because I'd let her read some of my poems that I still hadn't been able to find a French publisher for. Marie-Paule believed in me and asked if she could have some of her friends look at them. My mind was elsewhere. I was thinking of my country and of my mother, from whom I hadn't heard for a while. She had called me a couple of times, but this had been a great financial sacrifice. I learned to live and survive by telling myself that my thoughts were for her, only for her. Since we were in the midst of hard times—the Congolese government hadn't disbursed our scholarship funds for the past six months—I wasn't able to call her myself. When word reached her of my financial struggles, she'd found a way to send me some money. However, what turned out to be a substantial portion of her savings, once converted into French francs, had barely been enough for me to buy a sandwich. I was able to get one of my compatriots returning home to pass on a message and reassure her that I would figure things out and find some odd job or other in no time.

Using a friend's documents, I was able to find work in construction for a few days. Given my status as a foreign student, I would have needed to obtain authorization from the Labor Ministry, and this would only have been granted if I'd been able to submit a work contract, which was difficult to obtain. My roommates had been reminding me of late of my obligations, and since this job paid really well, I was able to pay my part of the rent on time, which meant that they now saw me in a favorable light.

A few days earlier, a French guy stopped me in front of a shop in the Place du Commerce. Bald, wearing a suit and tie, he'd handed me a leaflet from the Jehovah's Witnesses and promised he would visit me at home. True to his word, he did knock on my door the following Sunday and spent over an hour sharing the Word of God. Since he was the owner of a construction company, I leapt at the opportunity to ask him whether he might be able to hire me part-time. His good humor quickly dissipated. Clearly embarrassed, he apologized profusely.

"You know, things aren't that simple. We haven't been that busy lately. And in any case, you need experience to work construction ..."

I let him know I was ready to handle equipment or do anything else that didn't require special training. The man kept coming up with excuses, opened the Bible, and started reading passages about the heavenly kingdom. I didn't open the next time he knocked on the door. I also gave up looking for work and concentrated instead on my studies ...

I gradually adjusted to my new life as a student in spite of all the radical changes that had taken place. Back in the Congo, our attitude in class was far more "offensive." During oral presentations, for example, each of us did all we could to challenge those who were presenting. Our French classmates were very different, and one could gauge by the redness of their cheeks their anxiety when it came to public speaking. In addition, our way of speaking was constantly derided both in class and in the dining halls. People in France no longer used the imperfect subjunctive ... For us, this remained one of our most cherished tenses! The language spoken by the natives therefore seemed impoverished to us, corrupted by terrible laziness. These young people had learned French hanging on to their mother's skirts and taken, in our eyes, the most appalling shortcuts. Among these was the habit of bypassing tense sequences by hiding behind supposed evolutions in the language. How many times were we interrupted by one of our classmates shouting out at us:

"Hey, that's not how people speak these days! You sound like old fogeys!"

The journalist and writer Alain Schifres has railed against "today's French people," "those hexagonals," because of their attitude toward the way in which foreigners speak the language:

> A foreigner who speaks our language admirably well deserves the highest esteem. Speaking our language admirably well is seen as a tribute. "Admirable" means: better than oneself. In a literary manner. If we were to speak in that way we would sound somewhat ridiculous. But coming from a foreigner, the situation is fascinating. This admirable foreigner may once in a while get stuck on a word and we will delight in correcting them like we would a child: for if there's one thing we Hexagonals who speak no other language

sure enjoy doing, it's correcting the mistakes the francophone foreigner makes. With the patience the master has for an attentive pupil. With the paternalism of the land owner or the fierceness of the poor white settler. And often yelling at them: the foreigner doesn't hear well![1]

We were saddened by this attitude, especially since we'd already endured the whip just for failing to form a past participle correctly. And then, because we hadn't learned French at home, where our parents all spoke different Congolese languages, we'd only discovered it in books. As a result, how could we avoid "sounding like books"? We therefore had to tone it down a notch so that we wouldn't sound too old-fashioned. And young French people, humiliated by our perfectionism—especially in the presence of girls who, for the most part, were admirers—could only scorn our "Congolese" accents, or imitate us sarcastically by rolling the *R*s. It was obvious to us where weakness lay and we succeeded in not letting ourselves be thrown off. Whenever a so-called French person of "pure stock" is threatened by a foreigner in terms of language, mocking their accent is always their last resort. Of course, had we been born in France, the question of accent would not arise. It would have sufficed for these people to think a little about the effort it takes to learn and master "their" language, on top of all the other African languages we spoke, for them to alter their behavior. One does not speak a language better than someone else, no matter which language you have in mind, just because one has a more pleasant accent, but rather because one has learned how to play with the rules.

Once outside the confines of the university, we spoke among ourselves in our Congolese languages. I shared a rent-controlled apartment with four of my compatriots over toward the Boulevard des Anglais. We were all studying law, and two of us were working on a doctorate, one in maritime law and the other in public international law. We liked to head up to Paris to buy food products from our country and, on weekends, invite a few other Africans living in the area over to share a Congolese dish with us. We weren't, however, "closed off," and some French people also joined us to try the food they almost always described as "special and spicy." They'd push aside the sauce in search of a piece of meat, chew on some manioc, and marvel at the taste:

"Wow, that's very different, but really good!"

We shared the same goals: finish our studies and return to the Congo and serve our country, because they'd provided us with the means to pursue our studies thousands of miles away from home. We wandered around the town. In the evenings, we would hang out at Samba, an African nightclub where we would run into a few of the celebrities on the local soccer team.

A year later, the Congo had completely forgotten about us. The scholarships had yet to be disbursed. An "elder" taught us a trick to get through these hard times: it consisted in opening two separate bank accounts, both with overdraft facilities. You withdrew funds from the first account and only spent half of them. Then, when the time came to pay it back, you took money out of the second account and paid off the balance in the first. Reimbursing funds in this manner showed the bank you were a dependable client, and they would then authorize an increase in your overdraft limit. This cavalry worked for a while, at least until both accounts ended up in the red, at which point the respective establishments would freeze your account and on top of it all issue a prohibition on banking. The only thing left for us to do was to send out distress calls to our embassy in Paris. When the latter even deigned to respond, it was merely to promise us that we could expect a payment for two months out of the twelve that were already overdue. Even when this small advance came through, it was barely enough to cover the rent and allow us to pick up a few odds and ends. A few of us ended up taking up refuge over at our French girlfriends'.

Basically, we had only one idea in mind: to leave Nantes and move to Paris. Everything seemed possible in Paris. And to top it off, there was a sizeable Congolese community living there. I was obsessed by the idea and midway through the year decided to interrupt my studies and to resume them later at the University of Paris IX–Dauphine.

Paris-Dauphine may not have been the Sorbonne, but its prestige was such that I was able to come to terms with my childhood dream. Seventeen of us were enrolled in the graduate seminar on economic and social law. Even though my fellow students were all White, the question of skin color disappeared overnight. We'd all been through a drastic selection process just to be admitted to this institution. In fact, the university had been criticized a few years earlier for its selection process which many saw as unconstitutional, behaving as if they were one of the select *Grandes écoles*. For the first time, I caught myself thinking that if there was any justice in France, it was to found in the higher education system. Whites had tried and failed to be admitted, whereas I now found myself in this small group after an oral exam in which only my knowledge of French law, and not my accent, had mattered. Many of my fellow students became attorneys, insurance underwriters, or brokers on the Paris stock exchange. As for me, I worked for the multinational Suez-Lyonnaise des Eaux for a decade or so before leaving for the United States, where I'd been presented with an opportunity to teach francophone African literatures. This offer came at a time when I was devoting more of my time to writing, and some of my books were already being taught in American universities.

It would, nevertheless, be wrong to say, as my African brothers all too eager to knock France often do, that France abandoned me and that the United States welcomed me with open arms. I was making a decent living in France and I very well could have continued in this way for the rest of my life. This was first and foremost a very personal decision, one made after mature reflection. If I accepted to teach in the United States, this was because I knew deep down this wouldn't mean cutting myself off from this language I consider my own and in which I continue to write: French. In fact, I insisted on teaching in French when I first arrived—something I still do to this day. I also made it a point to teach, beyond the African authors, a number of French authors I really liked. I was, in spite of myself, going to become an ambassador of sorts for a culture and language which colonialism had handed down to me. In a roundabout way, teaching African authors of French expression to American students made it possible for me to spread the French language. And it was in America that I was first categorized as a French author, because in that country one's skin color is not automatically equated with an individual's country of origin. Because I speak and teach *in* French, Americans assume I must *be* French. It would never cross their mind to ask me whether I was "Franco-something."

8 Bound to Violence

LET US GO back to Nantes. My application to the Sorbonne had arrived after the deadline, which I certainly regretted. However, these feelings soon dissipated when I realized what this city represented for me—and for Black people in general—a city to whose university I'd been accepted. I stared at the passersby and wondered whether they were aware of what this city symbolized. The oldest and most historic buildings were like witnesses to a past that was obviously not taught with any degree of objectivity. I went in search of self-discovery on every street corner, looking for a component of my identity. Nantes is one of those places my ancestors transited through, in the eighteenth century, during the slave trade, and the city owes a great deal of its prosperity to the commerce between Africa, Europe, and the Americas, an enterprise better-known as the "Triangular trade," "Atlantic slave trade," or "Western slave trade." On otherwise quiet streets, I had the impression of hearing murmurings, voices that never stopped crying for justice. Life continued, and modernity imposed other priorities. I could very well have given this no further thought, but circumstances were such that all francophone sub-Saharan Africans, much like the French state itself, even if unwittingly, are compelled to remember this history. As it so happens, any francophone sub-Saharan African wishing to obtain French nationality is required to obtain a copy of his birth certificate in this city. A bit like going back to square one! Stepping into the municipal registry office was comparable to entering a morgue to identity a corpse. That was the price one had to pay to be recognized in this country.

Throughout the nineteenth century, most of Nantes' mayors had been slave traders, but the city was far from being the only one to shoulder this heavy responsibility. I certainly would not want to appear to be letting Nantes off the hook, but one could also mention cities such as Le Havre, Bordeaux, Saint-Malo, or La Rochelle, which actively participated in the Triangular trade. Nonetheless, it would not be accurate to say that Whites alone captured Blacks to reduce them into slavery.

The role played by Blacks in the slave trade remains a taboo subject to this day among Africans who refuse to look at themselves in the mirror. The mere mention of this history is tantamount to committing a felony and will not fail to lead to accusations of playing into the hands of the West and contributing to negationism. Our silence when it comes to the question of our participation is something in which we share responsibility. Either one remains silent or spews forth platitudes meant to perpetuate the image of an Africa shamelessly decapitated by Europe. Yet, the participation of those that are labeled the "African slave traders" is not an invention aimed at consoling Europe and appeasing "the White man's tears." Perhaps this is why Olivier Pétré-Grenouilleau's book that dealt with this issue was so harshly criticized by Africans?[1] Do we still have to continue denying Black slaves were rounded up and taken to the coast by other Blacks and Arabs during the era of slavery? This "ambiguity" explains the latent conflict in evidence today between Africans and Antilleans and, further afield, African Americans. For the most part, these "other Black brothers" blame Africans for having collaborated in this evil trade with the complicity of tribal chiefs.

Something that happened in the United States in 2003 definitively convinced me that the legacy of slavery remains a gaping wound in what is known as the Black world. Since that day, I speak differently to an African than I do to an African American.

I was living in the town of Ann Arbor (Michigan) at the time, and on a road trip to Washington, DC, with two friends of mine, the one a mixed-race Franco-American and the other an African American. The former, Pierre, was working on his dissertation on the work of the writer of Haitian origin Dany Laferrière. His father, an African American, had participated in the landing in Normandy. His mother was French. Pierre had lived for a while in France before moving in with his father in the United States. Raised in two cultures, something he felt proud of, he was a fairly quiet, likeable guy, who had some very reasonable and balanced views on the "racial question." Blacks thought of him as White, and the reverse was true when he was among Whites. As he would say with a mischievous grin, there wasn't anything surprising about this given that this was precisely the "status" of a mixed-race person. Pierre had introduced me to Tim, an African American who was a garbage collector in Ann Arbor. Unlike Pierre, Tim was extremely bothered by the conditions of Blacks in America and would not let anything pass when he talked about what he considered the "supreme cause." I therefore found myself caught between two "types" of African descendants, two examples of what the diaspora had yielded: a cross between a White and an African American, and a descendant of African slaves who had come to America via the slave trade. From my point of view, it was almost as if I was the incarnation of their "roots," "deepest Africa," and of the Black person that had never experienced slavery. We all lived in the same neighborhood, and occasionally Pierre and I would go and watch a football game over at Tim's. He overflowed with kindness, and in jest nicknamed me "Mandingo." I attributed this joke to his romanticized view of Africa, since he'd once shared with me his obsession for the Mandingo people. Even so, the image he had of contemporary Africa was extremely negative. He kept alluding to barbarism, famine, civil wars, and dictatorships. In a word, all the things reported in the news. He'd never set foot on the Black continent, and so as far as he was concerned we still lived in mud huts and continued to subsist on the land or by hunting. Which explained the dual meaning of the term "Mandingo." His obsession for the Mandingo people was no doubt due to Alex Haley's book *Roots: The Saga of an American Family*, published in 1976, but most likely also to the television adaptation *Roots* a year later. The series enjoyed worldwide success and helped awaken the pride of Africans, in particular those who'd been making the case to the West for reparations for slavery for decades.

The African American author had traveled to Gambia, "the land of his ancestors," to improve his understanding of his origins. While visiting a small village, he'd met a *griot* who recounted the genealogy and history of his bloodline all the way up until the figure of Kunta Kinte, an old Mandingo captured by Whites when he left the village to chop wood to make a drum. He finally landed in Virginia after several months at sea, a crossing that saw numerous Africans perish. Kunta Kinte would be the starting point for a long line of slaves who faced a tragic fate, yet who would be determined to make a place for themselves in America.

Calling me "Mandingo" was thus a way for Tim to remind me surreptitiously of my barbarism, the kind which, apparently, had driven my ancestors, less courageous and dignified than Kunta Kinte, to commit an irreparable deed: selling one's own brothers to the Whites.

We'd made reservations at a small hotel in the city center in Washington so that we could attend Pierre's brother's wedding. He was quite a bit older than him, born from the relationship of his father with an African American woman. Someplace else, people would have spoken of half-brothers, but Pierre preferred to simply call him "my brother."

"That's how it is in Africa," he insisted.

The wedding wasn't until the next day, and so we decided to go and party at Zanzibar, an African nightclub. Tim had already had a few glasses of whiskey back in his hotel room by the time we decided to head out on the town. He was the one who'd suggested we go and do some "African dancing" to get back to our roots:

"When I listen to African music, it's as if I was back home. Well, tonight, I want to go back home!"

Pierre was in the driver's seat and Tim sat down next to him in the front, while I got in the back. I was sure he'd nodded off—his chin was resting against his chest—when the African American suddenly sat up and started ranting:

"Africa's a pile of shit!"

I burst out laughing, but his jokes soon turned into personal attacks against me:

"Hey, Mandingo, I bet it feels good to be out of the African bush? I bet you're happy to be driving around in a nice American car and to be working in a university in my country, eh?"

Since I wasn't responding, he raised his voice:

"Hey, I'm talking to you Mandingo! You could at least answer the son of a slave, or does your rank as the chief of an African tribe prevent you from doing that?"

Pierre did his best to calm him down, but Tim was completely beside himself:

"No, Mandingo has to answer me! I'm tired of keeping my mouth shut, he owes me an explanation!"

"Come on Tim, don't you think you're going a bit too far?" Pierre asked, slowing the car down a little.

"No, I don't. This Mandingo comes to my country, he's given a good job in a major university, and I'm stuck in a crap job just like back in slave days! Him and his ancestors sold me to the Whites and it's his fault I'm nothing more than a bedbug in America today! If he hadn't sold me, I'd still be in Africa, and even if I were poor, at least I'd be free! I'm gonna kill him! I swear Pierre, I'm gonna kill him!"

Pierre and I really didn't know what to do. Tim was so angry his eyes were now bloodshot, and the fierce look he gave me betrayed deep-seated hatred.

I asked Pierre to pull over so that I could get out of the car, but this just made matters worse.

Tim started shouting at the top of his lungs:

"You're not going anywhere, I'm gonna kill you!"

He turned toward me, and in a split second, his long arms reached out to grab my neck. I moved back as far as I could in my seat and the car started swerving.

Pierre pulled over on the hard shoulder and I jumped out of the vehicle. Pierre wasted no time driving away while Tim was still screaming.

"I'm gonna kill you, you filthy African!"

I got a cab back to the hotel. I went up to my room, packed my bag, and went to find another hotel in the area. Early the next morning, Pierre told me how the rest of the evening had gone. When they got back from Zanzibar, Tim had gone several times to knock on the door of what had been my room. Pierre had asked him to go and apologize. But before that, Tim had said he was going to get a gun and shoot me!

I spotted Tim in the crowd at the wedding. He was avoiding me and seemed really embarrassed, clearly unsure what attitude to adopt toward me. Pierre intervened so that we could make peace.

Tim apologized profusely once we got back to Michigan. He wasn't sure what had come over him, claiming that he'd fallen prey to evil spirits. I accepted his apology, but needless to say, things were never quite the same again after that night.

I am only too aware of what an African can expect in assuming their share of the responsibility for the slave trade. When the brilliant Malian writer Yambo Ouologuem published his novel *Le devoir de violence* in 1968, it wasn't long before the guillotine came down.[2] In this work, which recounts the legend of the Saifs and their rule of the kingdom of Nakem (one should not forget that this is a work of "historical fiction"), the author reminds us that the enslavement of Africans by Arabs and "African notables" existed a long time before the Europeans arrived. Colonization and slavery were thus not "inventions" that came from outside of Africa or that coincided with the appearance on the continent of the "pale faces."

The summary of the novel on the back cover of the 1968 edition breaks with the taboo in no uncertain terms: "It is the fate of the Negro to have been baptized in suffering: first by the colonialism of African notables, then by the Arab conquest. The book covers eight centuries (1202–1900) and is composed of a fresco, a chronicle, a contemporary novel, and drama.... The Whites played the game of the African notables ..." Assuming our share of responsibility was what Ouologuem was inviting us to do. But instead, "Our eyes drink the brightness of the sun and, overcome, marvel at their tears. *Mashallah? Wa bismillah!*,"[3] laments the author in that incantatory way that is the long-standing hallmark of his work.

Ouologuem's novel announced the birth of a "new African literature," unfettered and removed from consensual themes. It also heralded the emergence of self-critique, a prerequisite for legitimacy in the process of reproaching others. This was a daring and bold move at a time when African writers were expected to blindly celebrate African civilizations and portray a continent where everything was calm and peaceful prior to the arrival of the European villains; the favorite scapegoats used to explain away the stalemate characteristic of African states after independence, from the late 1950s on. Universally acclaimed, Ouologuem's novel was the first by a francophone sub-Saharan African author to be awarded one of France's major autumn literary prizes. But the author's troubles were only just beginning: his publisher withdrew the book from circulation following a controversy in which it was alleged the Malian had plagiarized works by Graham Greene and André Schwarz-Bart. In any event, this remains one of the rare instances in which a work accused of plagiarism, but about which no official complaint was ever formally made, was removed from book shops by its publisher at the precise time when France hoped to discover a new literary genius. Nevertheless, the novel has enjoyed an enviable track record abroad. Included on syllabi the world over—principally in American universities—*Bound to Violence* remains one of the incontrovertible works in the history of African literature of French expression, to be read alongside Ahmadou Kourouma's *The Suns of Independence*, Sony Labou Tansi's *Life and a Half*, and Henri Lopes' *The Laughing Cry*.[4]

After the suspicions of plagiarism, Ouologuem became a pariah and did not publish any new work, with the exception of an incendiary pamphlet in 1969, arguably one of the most highly corrosive texts on the Black presence in France: *Lettre à la France nègre*. The silence of Africans during this whole affair, notably that of the champion of Négritude, Léopold Sédar Senghor, was deafening. Were they going to come to the defense of someone who had "deconstructed" the history of Africa with such a "duty of insolence"? Until 2003, the book was unobtainable in France, that is until Pierre Astier, the director of the Serpent à Plumes publishing house at the time, had the courage to rerelease it ...

9 The Identity Card

When people ask me how emigrating has influenced my writing, I'm unable to come up with any kind of concrete or definitive answer. This is most likely because I'm increasingly convinced that travel and border-crossing nourish my anxieties, help shape an imaginary which in the end resembles my homeland. My very own inner quest is at stake, my way of perceiving the universe. I made a conscious decision not to close myself off and to listen to the sound and the fury of the world, to never look at things as being fixed.

I did not become a writer because I emigrated. Then again, the perspective I had on my homeland did of course change once I moved away from it. In my earliest attempts at writing—all of which were I was still in the Congo—I always felt like something was missing, that my characters were somehow cloistered, that they had difficulty breathing and that they were clamoring for more space. Emigration helped strengthen the trepidation I carry deep inside, and that's the basis, I believe, for all creative activity. One writes because of the feeling that "something is not quite right," because of the urge to move mountains, to thread, as one might say, an elephant through the eye of a needle. Writing can simultaneously ground you, turn into a cry in the night or become an ear outstretched toward the horizon ...

Born in Africa, in the Congo-Brazzaville, I spent a good part of my youth in France before settling in the United States. Congo is where my umbilical cord is buried, France is the adopted homeland of my dreams, and America a corner from which I can observe the footsteps of my wanderings. These three geographic spaces are forever welded, and there are times when I forget on which continent I go to bed or on which I write.

My good friend and brother Dany Laferrière, with the vitality he's known for, keeps telling me that "writers should live in a city they don't like." I take this as an invitation to keep one's distance, almost as a permanent reinvention of that lost paradise, gone astray somewhere in our childhood memories. I love all these cities I travel through, and I'm always filled with wonder at just how different each place is from those in which I grew up. I'm buoyant when I arrive in a new place, and I try my hardest to clear my head of all thoughts. One cannot be an emigrant if one exports one's being, habits, customs, tastes, with the goal of imposing them on the country welcoming you. Only when the place in which you find yourself is so completely different to your "natural milieu" will childhood memories come surging to the surface, the clamor of the crowded street, the joys, but also the suffering of our people. The tornado season makes one truly appreciate the virtues of a clear blue sky, how awe-inspiring it can be when a bird takes flight, the essence of a blossoming flower for whose name one searches in vain until it suddenly hits you that the very same flower also grows back in Brazzaville in one of Moungali's public gardens. Standing in the desert, one realizes that the Atlantic Ocean and the Congo River are a divine blessing. Conversely, the risk would be to assume that an "emigrant's" words spring only from nostalgia. One can never leave home and yet still feel homesick. I'm not a very nostalgic person. Instead, I feel trepidation at the thought that I will one day leave this world without having unearthed the smallest detail that ties us together . . .

10 Literature of the Stomach

AT A TIME when a new form of "Africanism" is emerging, a number of francophone sub-Saharan African writers have been questioning the necessity of using the French language as a means of expression. Among these, the Cameroonian Patrice Nganang has gone as far as to propose "writing without France." A proposition—a demand, in fact, given that the author has stated that those who refuse to heed his call should be considered guilty of upholding colonial ideology. This is what he argues:

> Alas, writing without France means first and foremost to write beyond "la Francophonie." It means reclaiming the lateral mobility of our forefathers and mothers who used to move from one country or place to another, and from one language to the next, without having to first legitimize their movements. Who would move according to their necessity, speaking a language according to their location, with the same dexterity in medumba as in bassa or even douala: in short, they did not live the reality of their multiple languages as a curse, as Gaston-Paul Effa would have it, in line with purely colonial arguments, but rather as a *reality*.[1]

One has every right to ask whether this ideology of abandoning the French language does not potentially conceal an even more fundamental question: that which relates to *talent*, the one unit of measure when it comes to evaluating a writer no matter which language she or he decides to write in. Aren't African writers overlooking the real issue by launching themselves into such diatribes: *literature*? And when my colleague Patrice Nganang ponders a few lines later: "Will the day come when African writers will genuinely no longer be francophones?"[2] there can be little doubt that he has chosen to distance himself from the realm of creativity and gotten himself mired in the bickering of activism. How does being francophone prevent one from being a writer? Surely the shadow of France is not so cumbersome that it prevents us from writing in complete freedom? In a poem in which he paid homage to Aimé Césaire, the Congolese poet and historian Théophile Obenga reminded us of the African writer's state of mind with regard to the language of his former master: "The words may be theirs but the song belongs to us." And what could one say of the impertinence, the linguistic fugues of writers such as Ahmadou Kourouma, Patrick Chamoiseau, Sony Labou Tansi, or Daniel Biyaoula? If the adjective "francophone" in the term "francophone author" is too much for some, perhaps one should first begin by just being an "author"!

The main argument put forward by those who today would prefer to write "without France" is that the French language is tainted with a fatal, insurmountable, unforgiveable flaw: *it was the language of the colonizer.* That it is a language that prevents us from speaking with any kind of authenticity. "Authenticity"? Now there's another word charged with a whole range of unimaginable consequences. Was it not in the name of authenticity that some of the continent's nations drove their people to a state of deliquescence? As a matter of fact, it was during the 1970s that then president of Zaire Mobutu Sese Seko began the campaign that became known as "Zairianization," a policy that sought to revive "African authenticity" and rid the country of all lingering vestiges of Western influence. The dictator banned his people from wearing ties and imposed the "abacost" as the official national attire.[3] At the same time, place names inherited from the colonial era were replaced by new ones that had an African resonance. Leopoldville, the capital, thus became Kinshasa, and Elisabethville was changed to Lubumbashi. These policies were primarily aimed at reappropriating Zairian goods and wealth, measures which on the surface at least seemed commendable, especially at a time when the majority of African nations were turning to Communism. However, this did not prevent the ruling dictatorship from becoming one of the most ruthless on the entire continent, with a president obsessed with a cult of personality and solely preoccupied with the well-being of his own clan to the detriment of his people left to wallow in poverty. Mobutu claimed the country's wealth his own, all the while multiplying human rights violations, and this until his precipitous fall in 1997 after more than thirty years of absolute power.

According to the proponents of authenticity, the French language acts as a vehicle for various subservient "codes," turns of phrase unsuited to African phraseology that we would be wrong to underestimate. The Senegalese writer Boubacar Boris Diop, for example, after publishing several books in French (with L'Harmattan and Stock),[4] has said that henceforth he will write in Wolof: "For me, French—and English—is a ceremonial language, and there is something intimidating about its grammatical and cultural codes.... All the more reason why African writers may question the meaning and purpose of their writing."[5] Our fellow writer would indeed publish a novel entirely in Wolof in 2003, *Doomi Golo*,[6] but he followed this up shortly thereafter with *L'impossible innocence*, and one would be hard pressed to find a better example of both a classical and masterful usage of the French language.[7]

The whole situation becomes even more ambiguous when a French publisher decides to republish a book by an African author *in* Africa. This was the case with Diop's *The Knight and His Shadow*, a novel that was first published in Paris and then released in a more affordable paperback version in Africa, in French, designed for readers on the continent. The same happened with Cheikh Hamidou Kane's novel *Les gardiens du temple*.[8]

Better yet, Ngũgĩ wa Thiong'o's English-language publisher goes so far as to underwrite the publication of some of his books in Kenya but also in his native Kikuyu! So here we have the colonizer coming to the rescue of the colonized's language! I therefore ask myself the following crucial question: are writers such as V. S. Naipaul, Salman Rushdie, Zadie Smith, Derek Walcott, and Edwidge Danticat "inspired by colonial ideology" when they reveal the extent of their talent as writers in the English language? Unless, of course, these proponents of authenticity—in an attempt to deceive us with sophistry—don't actually consider the English language as originating from a colonial power...

In reality, however, Boubacar Boris Diop makes a subtle distinction between African writers who are "insiders" and those who are "outsiders." African writers who live in Europe are "outsiders" and more often than not seen as being out of touch with reality. Since they're cut off from their roots, the assumption is made that their worldview must necessarily be warped. Mired in the Parisian publishing establishment, these corrupt authors no longer touch the "hearts" of their African "brothers and sisters" but rather speak to the "reason" of their readers that apparently dictate what they write: "works written with a Western audience in mind," as the Senegalese journalist Nabo Sène has argued.[9]

By contrast, those African writers who reside in Africa, the "insiders," are the embodiment for the continuity of values and traditions, the "guardian of the tree," to borrow the title of one of the Cameroonian Jean-Roger Essomba's novels. Their main struggle then consists in freeing themselves from the chains of *francophonie*, the root of all that ails them. Their task is to reflect on the past, promote their languages, "write without France," "reclaiming" in the process "the lateral mobility of [their] forefathers and mothers," at the very moment when others are endeavoring to locate this mobility within far greater exchange networks, each language ultimately pecking away at another. Even when it comes to incredibly stylistically precise works by the Cameroonian Gaston-Paul Effa or the Chadian Nimrod—who both live in France—one would have to be hard of hearing (or unwilling to listen) not to detect the pulsating rhythms of the language.

When one fights for a cause, whatever it may be, the first thing one learns is to bracket one's ideas, to discipline oneself in order to set an example. To expect an African writer of French expression to cease being francophone and to substitute—as Patrice Nganang is ultimately suggesting—the anglophone model instead, is nothing less than an attempt to seduce an African youth in search of direction. Furthermore, to blame something on a situation from which one benefits oneself is, to say the least, rather disingenuous. Unless one practices a "literature of the stomach," of the kind that entails satisfying one's hunger before then complaining, all the while waiting for the next craving! We can indeed see that most of these people eager to preach, including those "insiders," have received sizeable dividends from *francophonie*. They're invited to literary festivals and book fairs and regularly apply for grants and writing residencies that are all funded by French institutions. After a bad experience with an African publishing house, many of them set out to find a Parisian one, beginning, as it so happens, with Patrice Nganang himself. And along the way, he was only too happy to pick up the Marguerite Yourcenar prize given in the United States with the support of the Consulate General of France! And while we are on the subject, let's just add that Jean-Paul Sartre was wrong to refuse the Nobel Prize. All this to say that the circumstances confronting a francophone sub-Saharan African author are not all that different from a French provincial French author whose dream is to make it into the catalogue of the prestigious Parisian publisher Gallimard.

To write without France? The majority of francophone sub-Saharan African authors, if they even have a mother tongue, are incapable of writing in it. Many of these languages are still oral languages. The governments in these countries should, of course, implement linguistic policies. But before this can happen, for starters, one would have to "establish" a grammar, even rethink it, harmonize it, and that's if it existed in the first instance. Academies would have to be opened, dictionaries published, journals established—in short, a colossal effort would have to be made to prepare people to move from orality—to which Africa is often reduced—to writing, while simultaneously relinquishing the tendency to pride oneself on the role an old person plays in cultural transmission. I have already said this elsewhere: if indeed when an old person dies in Africa it is the same thing as a library burning, then the question that remains is *which* old person and *which* library, since there are still plenty of old fools on this planet![10] Furthermore, there are no laws preventing one from translating the work of a francophone sub-Saharan African author into an African language. Cheikh Hamidou Kane's *Les gardiens du temple* was written in French and then subsequently translated into Wolof. The point is not just to write in an African language; one still has to prepare Africans to read the language in question in the same way as a French, Chinese, or Russian person prepares to read theirs.

But the challenges are even greater than one may initially think: the francophone sub-Saharan African writer is still, without being conscious of it, a native. "The status of 'native' is a neurosis introduced and maintained by the colonist in the colonized *with their consent,*" Jean-Paul Sartre had stressed in his introduction to Frantz Fanon's *The Wretched of the Earth*.[11] A good place to begin would probably be with the native's *consent*. After all, how can one not be moved by Derek Walcott's words that would seem to aptly summarize the extent of the current desperation of the African writer of French expression:

> Our bodies think in one language and move in another, yet it should have become clear, even to our newest hybrid, the black critic who accuses poets of betraying dialect, that the language of exegesis is English, that the manic absurdity would be to give up thought because it is white. In our self-tortured bodies, we confuse two graces: the dignity of self-belief and the courtesies of exchange.[12]

11   Phantom Africa

THE NEW GENERATION of francophone sub-Saharan African writers are often advised to read or reread the African classics, the implication being that there is nothing new about their work. Boniface Mongo-Mboussa has also indicated that "in art, originality, contrary to what we are often told, is a rare bird. One thinks one is innovating, but all too often unaware that one is in fact merely imitating an existing classic or illustrious stranger."[1] But such a position is really a surreptitious way of setting the elders against the young, and let's face it, a way of accusing the new generation of writers of spitting on Négritude and of trampling on the corpses of Senghor, Césaire, and Damas.

One should mention that Boniface Mongo-Mboussa focuses mostly on the *thematic dimension* of literary creation from francophone sub-Saharan Africa. But themes alone don't explain everything and often even distort the picture one has of a writer's universe or of literature itself. This is certainly true when it comes to the question of *immigration*, a theme that has been explored for quite some time in African letters and received considerable critical attention since the 1980s. Some critics have even categorized writers such as the Senegalese Fatou Diome, the Congolese Daniel Biyaoula, or the Cameroonian Jean-Roger Essomba as "immigration writers." And this simply because they write, publish, and live outside of the African continent and because their works deal simultaneously with France, Africa, and the status of foreigners in Europe. Odile Cazenave is one such critic, and her book *Afrique sur Seine* takes this approach.[2]

According to Boniface Mongo-Mboussa, although immigration has become the main theme for young writers, it was always already central to African literature, and he provides a sample list of works published from the 1930s on all the way through to the 1990s. But how can one ignore the fact that the way in which immigration is perceived has also changed drastically?

The "contemplative and moralizing" nature of yesteryear focused on the critique of French society's traditions and customs, their way of speaking, of blowing their noses, of walking swiftly down the street, as was the case in the Ivorian Bernard Dadié's 1959 novel *Un nègre à Paris*, in which the narrator Tanhoé Bertin describes in minute detail the habits of Parisians, in a similar manner to how Montesquieu had done previously in his *Persian Letters* back in 1721.[3] For Tanhoé Bertin, this journey is a mission of sorts that the entire African continent has entrusted him with, and to whom he is now accountable. Born in Africa, he is thrilled to be handed a ticket to Paris by a White man who can't believe he has never been there. To this day, this work provides one of the most insightful looks at the state of mind of Parisians on the eve of independence. Surely, though, the type of immigration found in Dadié's book differs considerably from the "immigration self-flagellation" in the Togolese author Sami Tchak's *Place des fêtes* published over forty years later.[4] Tchak's central protagonist is *born in France*. The fruit of immigration, of that "Black presence in France," he cannot grasp what is going on "over there," on the Black continent. He doesn't understand African ways of being, even finds the expected reverence somewhat cumbersome, such as his father's wish of being buried, at all costs, "over there." And so the young man rebels, refuses to carry the weight of traditions his progenitor expects him to pass on. He wants to be as free in his culture as he is in his sexuality. This work is thus no longer merely about a traditional voyage from Africa to Europe but rather and most importantly, *concerns the relationship between Africans and other Africans* in Europe, and in particular in France.

There is, therefore, a fundamental divergence between the kind of immigration found in the first francophone sub-Saharan African novels and what is to be found in the works of their successors. The characters in today's works are desperate. They are confronted with laws that did not exist back in 1937, at the time when the Senegalese Ousmane Socé published *Mirages de Paris*, and when, let us not forget, the majority of colonial subjects were considered French citizens and could easily travel to the mainland if only they had the means.[5] In those days, immigration merely concerned demagogues, and the French economy, ravaged by decades of global conflict, was desperately in need of labor.

Themes are not, as we can see, static in essence. One has to regularly *visit* and *revisit* them. Not a single year has passed since the end of World War II without a major novel being published in France on the theme of the Occupation or of Nazism. Does this preclude the originality of the works in question?

African writers of the so-called "new wave" are thus experiencing, as some would have it, an identity crisis, and in more recent years, a range of polemics between those who declare themselves to be *inherently* African and those who, while meeting with strong criticism from the latter, are attempting to open themselves up to the world, to offer *new ways of thinking about* Africa. Négritude has perhaps never been so relevant, even though a good number of intellectuals consider it to be fossilized, principally following the death of one of its founders, Léopold Sédar Senghor. Having said this, some continue to speak of ingratitude and have people believe that the new generation devote themselves to spitting on the tombs of their illustrious elders, the very people who made us what we are today: free human beings.

Who was it that said we needed to consecrate those who showed us the path? Who was it that said that the roar of Aimé Césaire's *Notebook of a Return to the Native Land* could no longer be heard beyond the mountains? Who, today, struck with "neuralgia" would opt to undergo "depigmentation"?[6] Ladies and gentlemen, it is not a case of sell-outs and flunkies on one side who are embraced at book fairs and the worthy and noble resistance fighters on the other who show up bearing certificates of Africanity handed out by God only knows what official body. And yet, hostile as they are to change, overwhelmed by the course of events, the self-proclaimed guardians of African authenticity, epigones of the geniuses of Négritude, remain convinced that they exalt Negro values better than Césaire, Damas, Senghor, Rabemananjara, Wright, or Du Bois! Almost as if they write by proxy, too afraid to speak in their own name. The vision they offer of Africa is at best a caricature, incapable as they are of freeing themselves and repeating anything else but the refrains inherited from the cotton plantations.

When it comes down to it, these *fanatics* essentially belong to a sect that refuses to admit that Africa is multiple, complex, and undergoing rapid transformation. They assume the right to dictate to others what they should do for no other reason than that they are Black and born in Africa. But it is not enough to be Black: one also needs to feel African and to understand what this sentiment means so as to be able to describe it to others. Does Africa actually exist? Does it mean the same thing to everyone?

The real priority today should be to express the world in all its cruelty, in all its mutations, at the risk of exasperating those who dream of a literature that sought only to glorify with one voice a distant, artificial Africa, a utopia outlined by the colonizer that is no longer ours. *That Africa does not exist.* That narrative is the product of a narrative skillfully woven over the years by those who enjoy reminiscing, a vision that stabs Africa right in the heart and with the full complicity of those guardians of authenticity for whom this vision is their stock and trade. By applauding this "phantom Africa," we disqualify ourselves and end up buttressing the prejudice that surrounds African letters ...

One may level accusations at young writers for wanting to blend into the mold of a global literature, one that would be less peripheral, more prestigious and rewarding, and thereby erase "those external signs of Africanness," summoning, and let's be clear about this, a kind of *universality.* We are told that only those who gain proximity to a Western notion of literature will ever achieve universality. One should not therefore be surprised that some writers, in order to attain this goal, believe it sufficient to remove all Black references from their texts, thereby avoiding any exoticism or risk of "sounding African." The point is not to sidestep speaking about Africa or to erase Africa from our creative work! But rather to counter the same old vision of Africa that has been served up to us for years, to turn down these surreptitious "commissions," these obligations whispered in the ears of African writers asking them to produce works that correspond to expectations, denying them the opportunity of choosing different avenues, different paths, and in the process harnessing their diversity. Otherwise, the prejudice toward African literature will not go away, and we should not then be surprised if people continue to repeat that African literature is a mere transcription of oral literature, or that African writers continue to be inspired by the stories they were told as children by an elder, guardian of memory and living library. *That Africa* does not exist, just as the literature that apparently stages it does not either. The main preoccupation of African writers is not their relationship with the Black continent, but first and foremost with literature, just like any other writer. *Is the Africa they write about, delineate, merely an empty shell, a prefabricated object*? To the extent that the primary readership for African literatures remains European—notably because of the price of books and distribution networks—how can one write in complete freedom, without the question of audience and of their fantasies and expectations being there at the back of one's mind?

Perhaps the time has come to rethink the very notion of Africa itself, and to move away from the idea of a fixed geography when it comes to the Black continent. What if, instead of a singular Africa, we spoke of *Africas*, a term the writer Henri Lopes had previously dared to use in his novel *Le chercheur d'Afriques* published by Seuil.[7]

Africa is no longer only in Africa. Africans are dispersed all over the planet and have created other Africas; they have tried their luck at other adventures that may prove to be beneficial to the cultural revitalization of the Black continent. Proclaiming "Africanity" is a form of fundamentalism, nothing less than sheer intolerance. How can a bird that has never left the branch on which it was born ever be able to hear the song of its companion migratory bird? We desperately need a confrontation, a showdown between cultures, regardless of where this actually takes place ...

12 The Suns of Independence

I WAS BORN after the suns of independence, but they were so incandescent, scorching all the African flora, draining the ground water and pushing the fauna back deep into the heart of the bush, that I inherited the complexion that reminds us of its glow, but more than anything else of the rejoicing, the everlasting effusions, while the voice of the Congolese musician Grand Kalle singing "Indépendance Cha Cha" rang out. I have seen many black-and-white photographs of this period. Pride was back. Blacks could come to terms with history, choose their own paths, no longer have to kowtow. In some of the photos my father showed me, I can still see Patrice Lumumba getting off a plane in Kinshasa and being met by a huge crowd. His heavy spectacles. His hair, with that distinct center parting. He'd just wrapped up talks with the Belgians. He wasn't scheduled to address the former colonial power, but he seized the opportunity, having jotted down a few notes while the others took their turn at the lectern. He's clearly furious, for on that 30th of June 1960, King Baudouin has essentially pronounced a paean to colonization according to which Belgium would have brought everything to the Congolese who in turn would have to be eternally grateful. Belgium itself would have decided on its own to accord Congo its independence. Lumumba chomps at the bit while the king speaks, and he begins to scribble more and more frenetically. He knows that the words he is about to utter will throw oil on the fire. He stands, surprising the protocol services, and exclaims:

> We have been the victims of ironic taunts, of insults, of blows that we were forced to endure morning, noon, and night because we were blacks.... Who can forget, finally, the burst of rifle fire in which so many of our brothers perished, the cells into which the authorities threw those who no longer were willing to submit to a rule where justice meant oppression and exploitation?

Obviously two very opposite ways of conceiving of history. On the one hand the colonizer, eager to justify his actions, and on the other the colonized, condemning them. A familiar situation: the hunter and the game will never see a hunting expedition in the same way.

But I can also make out the slightly faded image of Mobutu himself, standing right behind Lumumba, a man he would waste no time in assassinating with the help of Western nations. Too much excitement can diminish one's focus, and in our elation, we didn't take the time to realize we'd become our own masters only on paper. Some clever minds still stubbornly believe in complete African independence, and on paper at least, they're given the benefit of the doubt. Be that as it may, let us not forget that not everything that is printed is the truth. An independent being is in the first place someone who's chosen to define themselves and, as a consequence, to own this definition. Yet, when it comes to assuming responsibility, African independence has left more people sick than healthy, more ghost-states than well-functioning nations. And even when the most enthusiastic strike a chord for activism and the integrity of a sovereign Africa, the music surges from the remains of colonization. When the specter of a historic event continues to haunt one's conscience, the tendency is to seek refuge in myth—and it's a short step from myth to mythomania.

We dreamed for a long time about the suns of independence, and once these came about we closed our eyes, dazzled. When we opened them up again, our States looked like roaming shadows, governed by ogres whose appetite increased at the same rate as our anxiety.

For a continent that had endured the bleakest moments known to history, this was to be a time to stand up and hold our heads up high with dignity, to take our fate into our own hands. But instead of doing that, we spent our time drawing up an inventory. The former colonizer looked on with a smile. Our incompetence was a great boon to those who had recently lost large chunks of land and an abundance of riches. We'd forgotten that life is best built by conjugating our verbs in the present tense. We plunged head-first into a mad undertaking of our own making: compiling a balance sheet of all our Black values. We thus lived in the past, a past that was *naturally* glorious, in which there were no wars, no clashes, and over which a homogenous African people ruled—in other words, a complete delusion. A paradise that existed before the Whites arrived and that we had to endeavor to recover at all cost. We had to build traditional societies, rekindle the luster of the olden days, and in an upsurge of authenticity aimed at galvanizing the people, outfit ourselves in leopard skin. And if the government impoverished a country along the way, well then so be it, that was the fault of the Whites.

From this desire to bring our ills before the jury of conscience, we needed an accused. We found him standing right there in front of us: the White. In short, the White was to blame for our paralysis. The White had shattered our dreams, burned our Gods, changed our traditions and norms, emptied our countryside, and corrupted our cities that were now "cruel."

What additional arguments could we possibly have recourse to in order to better excuse our inertia? We still had plenty up our sleeves.

We were forced out of our *case à palabre*, our traditional meeting place, on the grounds that Enlightenment philosophy was more luminous.

We replaced our "African emotion" with "Hellenic reason."

We accepted that there was no such thing as Black thought.

After all, reason had to be White, and preferably even Aryan.

We were a lazy people.

Montesquieu had said it: the people in the South were weak like old men, whereas those in the North were more vigorous because of the cold climate. How could one deny this in the face of such evidence and in the pen of the greatest minds in Western philosophy? People in the North were all intelligent, handsome, and strong. Whereas the rest of us, born in the South, had "invented neither powder nor compass," "could harness neither steam nor electricity," and were among "those who explored neither the seas nor the sky."[1] It was down to us to shout *Urbi et Orbi*, that we were "those without whom the earth would not be the earth."[2] In 1939, in his *Notebook of a Return to the Native Land*, Aimé Césaire stood up to this epic challenge:

> And this land screamed for centuries that we are bestial brutes; that the human pulse stops at the gates of the slave compound; that we are walking compost hideously promising tender cane and silky cotton and they would brand us with red-hot irons and we would sleep in our excrement and they sell us on the town square and an ell of English cloth and salted meat from Ireland cost less than we did, and this land was calm, tranquil, repeating that the spirit of the Lord was in its acts.[3]

And if the poetic voice was too impenetrable for mere mortals, Césaire also wrote a "discourse" in which he argued that colonialism was necessarily a form of enslavement. Europe had committed one of the most heinous crimes in history by seeking to impose its view of the world on other peoples.

Now though, things gathered pace. The 1950s and 1960s announced the dawning of a new era. The Whites decamped by will or by force. Already, in 1947, the Malagasy Uprising had been witness to tens of thousands of deaths in a nationalist rebellion.

This proved contagious, and soon other French colonies would join in the fight: in 1954, Algeria launched an armed insurgency; meanwhile, Tunisia became independent two years later. By 1959, almost as many as ten African countries had become independent, and, by 1960, that number had doubled.

But despite that, the colonizer had a "Plan B": they had thought to "groom" the next generation of leaders. Men with *black skin* and *white masks*. Men who would "unconsciously" replace them but operate as their eyes and ears on the Black continent. Some of these men had fought for France in the world wars and defended the French empire. Others had been elected as representatives to the French parliament. And some would become presidents, while others were appointed as ministers, ambassadors, and so on. They even had French passports. And villas in Europe.

In sub-Saharan Africa, only Guinea had the courage to say no to France in a referendum they held in 1958, to the great displeasure of General de Gaulle, who had assumed that all Africans would, when given the opportunity to weigh in on their independence, inevitably demand protection from the empire. Guinea thus inaugurated a period of "ingratitude" toward France, and its president, Sékou Touré, now emerged as a Messiah of sorts, as someone who had had the nerve to stand up to a French statesman who measured almost six feet six and who had earned unquestionable respect for his war-time bravery.

And then, the names of "rebels" started to reverberate across the Black continent: Kwame Nkrumah, Patrice Lumumba … And behind these names, another ideology, links with other countries in the North, in particular the Soviet Union. But also, smaller Third World countries expressed their solidarity, with Cuba leading the way.

Independence was also a standoff between the traditional world and the modern world. Tie or no tie? Red wine or palm wine? French or

African languages? The White school or ancestral wisdom? It marked the beginning of the "ambiguous adventure." And, to a certain extent, we were not that far from the universe described in Ahmadou Kourouma's *The Suns of Independence*, in which the Malinké prince Fama, nostalgic for the grandeur of his family lineage, has to come to terms with a new way of life and, chiefly, the advent of the single party. Fama's disorientation in this new chaotic world exposes the state in which the formerly colonized found himself. Faced with the advent of what was considered modernity, what place would be given to tradition?

Our countries may very well have been decolonized on paper, but the "colonization of the mind," no doubt far more damaging, gnawed away at each individual. As such, we accepted in a quasi-systematic manner the grossly inaccurate image the colonizer had drawn of us. This "portrait of the colonized"—which remains palpable to this day— has conditioned the way in which we think to such a degree that there will always be someone who will claim that "things were better under colonial rule."

And what's more, African leaders have never based their policies around the question of conscience. Rather, they have been content with imitating the Western model of governance. Some heads of state, smitten by the cult of personality, stand today among the most comic but also demonic cast of characters—Idi Amin Dada, Jean-Bédel Bokassa, and Mobutu Sese Seko. It is hardly surprising that these megalomaniacs ended up in novels, in much the same way as their Latin American counterparts had previously.

Independence thus gave birth to the character of the dictator in francophone sub-Saharan African literature. But they also invented, in return, the figure of the rebel, as in Sony Labou Tansi's *Life and a Half*.

In no time at all, the suns of independence were clouded over in the African skies by forbidding dark clouds. The proliferation of ethnic conflicts, political assassinations, and "permanent coups d'états" have become facets of African life. The word "democracy" seems to have been banished from our leaders' vocabulary. Poverty on the continent now rivals the mineral wealth holdings in the hands of those who a short while ago were the masters. And when a country is brazen enough to set the record straight, the former colonial power manufactures an opponent from scratch, arms him, and supports him on his journey to power.

Future contracts are signed in the shelter of tents and to the ripple of gunfire. Never mind that some monarch installs himself in power for the next forty years or so or that his son succeeds him after he dies. Yes, this is indeed the new system in place for handing over power in Africa: from father to son. Some will even say that this was how things were done in many of the continent's traditional societies. Except that everyone forgets that this customary rule was democratically agreed upon by the people. We adopted constitutions that stipulated there be elections, yet very few African countries can claim a smooth functioning of the political process. In Gabon, Togo, and the Democratic Republic of the Congo, the sons of previous dictators have sustained the same devastating balance sheets as the fathers that sired them ...

We are accountable for our failure. We were unable to sever the Gordian knot and shoulder our responsibilities. Our silence and our inertia together allowed for the emergence of puppets who dragged the people into an abyss with the last genocide of the twentieth century, the one that unfolded before our very eyes, as the point of no return. This genocide was possible because we had integrated the image they had of us. Hutus: rough features, barbaric, imbecility. Tutsis: smooth features, intelligence, proximity with the civilized world. And while these "two camps" were busy killing each other, the West deployed its army on the fallacious pretext that it was protecting its nationals. At the UN, lengthy discussion was underway on a semantic point—was this genocide or not?—in the meantime, the massacres continued ...

In reality—and this is what stays in my mind from this disastrous half-century of purported autonomy—we are not the children of the suns of independence, we are the children of the post-Rwandan genocide. A genocide made possible by colonization and that has been perpetuated up until today thanks to all kinds of underhanded backdoor policies. Africa has never been as dependent as it is now on its masters and all at the expense of the people themselves. Beyond the blame that can be assigned to the West, Africans also have their place in the dock next to the accused ...

Appendix

This letter was written by Yaguine Koïta and Fodé Tounkara, both fourteen years old, stowaways found dead on August 2, 1999, in the landing gear of an airplane at Brussels International Airport.[1]

Conakry, Guinea, July 29, 1999

Excellencies, Messrs. members and officials of Europe,

We have the honorable pleasure and the great confidence in you to write this letter to speak to you about the objective of our journey and the suffering of us, the children and young people of Africa.

But first of all, we present to you life's most delicious, charming and respected greetings. To this effect, be our support and our assistance. You are for us, in Africa, those to whom it is necessary to request relief. We implore you, for the love of your continent, for the feeling that you have towards your people and especially for the affinity and love that you have for your children whom you love for a lifetime. Furthermore, for the love and meekness of our creator God the omnipotent one who gave you all the good experiences, wealth and ability to well construct and well organize your continent to become the most beautiful one and most admirable among the others.

Messrs. members and officials of Europe, we call out for your solidarity and your kindness for the relief of Africa. Do help us, we suffer enormously in Africa, we have problems and some shortcomings regarding the rights of the child.

In terms of problems, we have war, disease, malnutrition, etc. As for the rights of the child in Africa, and especially in Guinea, we have too many schools but a great lack of education and training. Only in the private schools can one have a good education and good training, but it takes a great sum of money. Now, our parents are poor and it is necessary for them to feed us. Furthermore, we have no sports schools where we could practice soccer, basketball or tennis. This is the reason, we,

African children and youth, ask you to create a big efficient organization for Africa to allow us to progress.

Therefore, if you see that we have sacrificed ourselves and risked our lives, this is because we suffer too much in Africa and that we need you to fight against poverty and to put an end to the war in Africa. Nevertheless, we want to learn, and we ask you to help us in Africa learn to be like you.

Finally, we appeal to you to excuse us very, very much for daring to write this letter to you, the great personages to whom we owe much respect. And do not forget it is to you whom we must lament about the weakness of our abilities in Africa.

Written by two Guinean children, Yaguine Koïta and Fodé Tounkara.

Notes

1. The Black Man's Tears

1. Pascal Bruckner, *The Tears of the White Man: Compassion as Contempt*, translated by William R. Beer (New York: Free Press, 1986).

2. Frantz Fanon, *Black Skin, White Masks*, translated by Richard Philcox (New York: Grove Press, 2008 [1952]), 204.

3. Fanon, *Black Skin, White Masks*, 202.

4. Fanon, *Black Skin, White Masks*, 203.

5. Fanon, *Black Skin, White Masks*, 205.

6. Alain Mabanckou, *Lettre à Jimmy* (Paris: Éditions Fayard, 2007), translated by Sara Meli Ansari as *Letter to Jimmy* (Berkeley, CA: Soft Skull, 2014).

2. A Negro in Paris

1. "Banania" products featured the image of a smiling African *tirailleurs* infantryman apparently thrilled with his exposure to French universalism. The poet Léopold Sédar Senghor denounced this marketing campaign, hailing, "I will tear down those Banania smiles from the walls of France," "Poème liminaire," in *Œuvre poétique* (Paris: Seuil, 1990), 7.

2. Régis Debray, *Les masques* (Paris: Gallimard, 1987), 238.

3. The Spirit of the Laws

1. This chapter is a revised version of the preface I wrote to the book *La France noire. Trois siècles de présences*, edited by Pascal Blanchard, Sylvie Chalaye, Éric Deroo, Dominic Thomas, and Mahamet Timera (Paris: La Découverte, 2011).

2. Occasionally, when I am lecturing in the United States, I like to play on the abbreviation USA and say instead "United Statistics of America."

3. Amin Maalouf, *In the Name of Identity: Violence and the Need to Belong*, translated by Barbara Bray (New York: Arcade Publishing, 2000), 164.

4. Murderous Identities

1. Michel Houellebecq, *La carte et le territoire* (Paris: Flammarion, 2010), translated by Gavin Bowd as *The Map and the Territory* (London: William Heinemann, 2011).

2. Olivier Luciani, cited in the *Dictionnaire de la France coloniale*, edited by Jean-Pierre Rioux (Paris: Flammarion, 2007), 71.

3. Yves Bénot, "La décolonisation de l'Afrique française," in *Le livre noir du colonialisme. XVIᵉ-XXIᵉ siècle: de l'extermination à la repentance*, edited by Marc Ferro (Paris: Robert Laffont, 2003), 517.

4. *Dictionnaire historique de la langue française*, edited by Alain Rey (Paris/LE ROBERT, 2010), 1774.

5. Jean-Claude Kauffman, *L'invention de soi. Une théorie de l'identité* (Paris: Armand Colin, 2004).

6. Kauffman, *L'invention de soi*, 1.

7. Cordélia Bonal and Laure Équy, "L'identité nationale selon Sarkozy," *Libération*, November 2, 2009.

5. Road to Europe

1. The full letter is included in an appendix.

2. SAPE is an acronym for the Société des ambianceurs et des personnes élégantes (The Society of Elegant Persons). Launched by the Congolese of Brazzaville, this movement considers clothing on the same level with "religion," and was popularized by musicians from the Democratic Republic of Congo (Papa Wemba, Emeneya Kester, and Koffi Olomidé, among others).

3. Daniel Biyaoula, *L'impasse* (Paris: Présence Africaine, 1996) and Jean-Roger Essomba, *Le paradis du nord* (Paris: Présence Africaine, 1996).

6. How Can One be Persian?

1. According to the *Panorama de l'Union européenne. Annuaire Eurostat 2000, le guide statistique de l'Europe, données 1992–2002* (Communauté européenne, 2004).

2. Quoted in *Le Figaro Magazine*, April 18, 2011.

3. Éric Zemmour speaking on the television show "Salut les Terriens," hosted by Thierry Ardisson and broadcast on Canal + on March 6, 2010.

4. Robert Ménard speaking on RTL radio's "On refait le monde," hosted by Christophe Hondelatte, and broadcast on March 21, 2011.

5. Robert Ménard and Emmanuelle Duverger, *Vive Le Pen!* (Béziers: Mordicus, 2011).

6. Marie Guichoux, "Dans les filets de Marine?," *Le Nouvel Observateur*, March 31, 2011.

7. The Foreign Student

1. Alain Schifres, *Les hexagons* (Paris: Le Livre de poche, 1996), 292–3.

8. Bound to Violence

1. Olivier Pétré-Grenouilleau, *Les traites négrières. Essai d'histoire globale* (Paris: Gallimard, 2004).
2. Yambo Ouologuem, *Le devoir de violence* (Paris: Seuil, 1968); *Bound to Violence*, translated by Ralph Manheim (London: Heinemann, 1971).
3. Ouologuem, *Bound to Violence*, 3.
4. Ahmadou Kourouma, *Les soleils des indépendances* (Montreal: Presses Universitaires de Montréal, 1968 and Paris: Seuil, 1970), translated by Adrian Adams as *The Suns of Independence* (New York: Africana Publishing, 1981), Sony Labou Tansi, *La vie et demie* (Paris: Seuil, 1979), translated by Alison Dundy as *Life and a Half* (Bloomington: Indiana University Press, 2011), and Henri Lopes, *Le pleurer-rire* (Paris: Présence Africaine, 1982), translated by Gerald Moore as *The Laughing Cry: An African Cock and Bull Story* (London: Readers International, 1987).

10. Literature of the Stomach

1. Patrice Nganang, "Writing Without France," in *Words and Worlds: African Writing, Literature, and Society: A Commemorative Publication for Eckhard Breitinger*, edited by Susan Arndt and Katrin Berndt (Trenton, NJ, and Asmara: Africa World Press, 2007), 237.
2. Nganang, "Writing Without France," 237.
3. The word "abacost" means "down with the suit" (a contraction of the French "à bas le costume"), a short-sleeved variation of the Chinese Mao suits.
4. Boubacar Boris Diop, *Le temps de Tamango* (Paris: L'Harmattan, 1981), *Les traces de la meute* (Paris: L'Harmattan, 1993), *Le cavalier et son ombre* (Paris: Stock, 1997), and *Murambi, le livre des ossements* (Paris: Stock, 2000). Some of these works are also available in English: *The Knight and His Shadow*, translated by Alan Furness (East Lansing: Michigan State University Press, 2015) and *Murambi, The Book of Bones*, translated by Fiona Mc Laughlin (Bloomington: Indiana University Press, 2016).
5. Jean-Marie Volet, interview, "À l'écoute de Boubacar Boris Diop, écrivain," *Mots pluriels*, no. 9 (1999) http://www.arts.uwa.edu.au/MotsPluriels/MP999bbd.html.
6. Boubacar Boris Diop, *Doomi Golo* (Dakar: Papyrus, 2003). The book was translated into French as *Les Petits de la guenon* (Paris: Philippe Rey, 2009) and English by El Hadji Moustapha Diop as *Doomi Golo: The Hidden Notebooks* (East Lansing: Michigan State University Press, 2016).
7. Boubacar Boris Diop, *L'impossible innocence* (Paris: Philippe Rey, 2004).

8. Cheikh Hamidou Kane, *Les gardiens du temple* (Paris: Stock, 1997).

9. Nabo Sène, "Des sociétés africaines morcelées," *Le monde diplomatique* (January 2003), 30.

10. Alain Mabanckou, *Écrivain et oiseau migrateur* (Brussels, Belgium: André Versaille éditeur, 2011).

11. Jean-Paul Sartre, "Preface," in Frantz Fanon, *The Wretched of the Earth*, translated by Richard Philcox (New York: Grove Press, 2004), liv.

12. Derek Walcott, "What the Twilight Says," in *What the Twilight Says: Essays* (London: Faber & Faber, 1998), 27.

11. Phantom Africa

1. Boniface Mongo-Mboussa, *Désir d'Afrique* (Paris: Gallimard, 2001), 22.

2. Odile Cazenave, *Afrique sur Seine: A New Generation of African Writers in Paris* (Lanham, MD: Lexington Books, 2005).

3. Bernard Dadié, *Un nègre à Paris* (Paris: Présence Africaine, 1959), published in English as *An African in Paris*, translated by Karen Hatch (Urbana: University of Illinois Press, 1994).

4. Sami Tchak, *Place des fêtes* (Paris: Gallimard, 2001).

5. Ousmane Socé, *Mirages de Paris* (Paris: Nouvelles Éditions Latines, 1937).

6. Léon-Gontran Damas, one of the founders of Négritude, was the author of several influential volumes of poetry, including *Pigments* (Paris: Guy Lévis Mano, 1937 and Présence Africaine, 1962) and *Névralgies* (Paris: Présence Africaine, 1966), invoked playfully in this passage by Alain Mabanckou.

7. Henri Lopes, *Le chercheur d'Afriques* (Paris: Seuil, 1990).

12. The Suns of Independence

1. Clayton Eshleman and Annette Smith, eds., *Aimé Césaire: The Collected Poetry* (Berkeley and Los Angeles: University of California Press, 1983), 64–6.

2. Eshleman and Smith, *Aimé Césaire: The Collected Poetry*, 67.

3. Eshleman and Smith, *Aimé Césaire: The Collected Poetry*, 61.

Appendix

1. The letter initially appeared in several media outlets, is available at www.Childsrights.org, and the English translation of the original imperfect French published at https://en.m.wikipedia.org/wiki/Yaguine_Koita_and _Fodé_Tounkara.

ALAIN MABANCKOU is a Franco-Congolese author and Professor of French and Francophone Studies at the University of California, Los Angeles. His novels include *Blue White Red, African Psycho, Broken Glass, Memoirs of a Porcupine, Black Bazaar, Tomorrow I'll Be Twenty,* and *The Lights of Pointe-Noire.* Shortlisted for the Man Booker International Prize in 2015, he is the recipient of numerous literary prizes, such as the Grand Prix Littéraire de l'Afrique noire, Prix Renaudot, Prix Georges Brassens, and the Grand Prix de Littérature Henri Gal from the Académie Française for his life's work.

DOMINIC THOMAS is Madeleine L. Letessier Professor of French and Francophone Studies at the University of California, Los Angeles. His books include *Nation-Building, Propaganda, and Literature in Francophone Africa; Black France: Colonialism, Immigration, and Transnationalism;* and *Africa and France: Postcolonial Cultures, Migration, and Racism.*

Printed in the USA
CPSIA information can be obtained
at www.ICGtesting.com
LVHW091301310824
789807LV00002B/71

9 780253 035837